Australian Biographical Monographs

6

Australian Biographical Monographs
Series Editor: Scott Prasser

Australian Biographical Monographs

6

Robert Menzies
Man or Myth

Scott Prasser

Connor Court Publishing

Published in 2020 by Connor Court Publishing Pty Ltd

Connor Court Publishing Pty Ltd
PO Box 7257
Redland Bay QLD 4165
sales@connorcourt.com
www.connorcourt.com
Phone 0497-900-685

Printed in Australia

ISBN: 9781925826906

Front cover design: Maria Giordano

Front cover picture: Wikipedia Commons.

"The most fundamental task in front of us is to educate a new generation, not for mere money-making or to comply with the law, but for an enlightened citizenship based upon honest thinking and human understanding."

-ROBERT G MENZIES, 16 October, 1942.

Australian Biographical Monographs

Series overview

The Connor Court Publishing's Australian Biographical Series on past leading Australian political leaders and other important figures seeks to provide an overview for those who are unfamiliar with the subject and to highlight the person's particular importance, controversies and contributions to Australia's progress.

The monographs are scholarly rather than academic in focus placing emphasis on a clear narrative, but with careful attention to referencing to ensure views expressed are supported by appropriate sources and evidence.

The Series was initiated because of the decline in the study of Australian history at our schools and universities and the consequential lack of knowledge or even worse, distorted views of some of Australia's leading figures who deserve to be remembered, understood for both their achievements, and as each volume also highlights, their flaws.

This monograph by Dr Scott Prasser on Sir Robert Menzies, provides a further perspective on Australia's longest serving and most successful prime minister.

Menzies deserves our attention. He has been undervalued and often derided by academia and even sometimes overlooked by the Liberal Party, the party he founded which has become Australia's most successful political party. He sustained it with a genuine philosophy based on individual effort supplemented by practical government action. In his sixteen years in office, he led the nation through difficult and uncertain times, helped it adjust to changing international circumstances, and laid the basis of modern Australia. Menzies and his governments were untainted by any allegations of corruption or scandal. This volume demolishes the myths that Menzies merely "presided" over Australia's post World War Two economic prosperity and that his political ascendency was a foregone conclusion aided by an inept opposition and a disengaged public. Rather, Menzies' success and Australia's great progress reflected his great political skills and his judicious policy choices. Scott has worked in both academia and in senior policy roles in both Commonwealth and state governments. From 2013-2019 he was Senior Adviser to three senior federal cabinet ministers that gave him insights into how governments work.

Introduction

Robert Gordon Menzies was Australia's longest serving and therefore our most politically successful prime minister. In fact, he held the prime-ministership twice – from 1939 to 1941, and then more impressively, uninterrupted from 1949-1966 – a total of 18 years, 5 months, and 12 days. During that second period Menzies won seven elections in a row. No-one at the national level had ever had such success, and no-one, for a variety of reasons, will achieve that again. Indeed, there will never be another Menzies. Moreover, despite this long time as prime minister, Menzies achieved one other distinction – he left office in January 1966 of his own accord, at a time of his own choosing. Menzies was not pushed, encouraged to go, suffering any dotage, or whispered against by his own colleagues. Nor did any scandal or political miscalculation force his decision. Only two other Australian prime ministers had achieved that previously,[1] and none since, as recent events testify. Few other national leaders in western democracies during the same period or since have enjoyed such a dignified exit. Nor did Menzies have to scheme and connive to hold on to his position like Adenauer of West Germany did during the 1960s.[2]

While a brief overview of Menzies' life and career is outlined, the prime focus of this short monograph is to outline, and critically assess, the issues and myths about Menzies especially during his second term as prime minister.

Issues and myths about Menzies

A key issue about Menzies is that despite his longevity in office, his stature as prime minister has been, until relatively recently, less assured on several counts.

First, Menzies' unsurpassed political success although applauded by many as a hallmark of his stature, electorate support, political skills, leadership, and sheer resilience, has been more railed against than praised by his critics. It has been explained as being easily achieved thanks not to Menzies' abilities or electoral appeal, but to other factors like: the international post World War Two economic boom; the biased electoral system; the disunited Labor opposition, and his manipulation of 'Cold War' fears, especially seen in relation to the Petrov spy defection (see later). As historian. F.G. Clarke summed up, Menzies was a "supreme political opportunist appealing to the Australian electorate time after time on a rabidly anti-Communist platform" and worse "aside from keeping himself in power does not seem to have believed in anything much".[3]

Second, Menzies' length in office was considered by some as not only too long, but one of missed opportunities, that lacked vision and held Australia back – though from what is never specified. Menzies and his Coalition did not govern Australia, they just presided as academic Donald Horne said in 1965:

> It was a feature of Menzies' long rule that little of
> what he did seems to matter much. His great talent
> was to preside over events and look as though as

if he knew what they were all about. His few active interventions proved mainly failures ... He seemed to believe that only he could run Australia ... Within his party he soon cut off from power or silenced all those who disagreed with him ... He was lazy in his reading and – despite the projection of an image of learning and culture – the truth is that he was not particularly well-read ... He used his power to little purpose.[4]

Only a few days after Menzies' death in 1978 Horne repeated his vituperative critique:

The television rhapsodies on Menzies, the day of his death, gave the show away. They couldn't come to grips with what exactly they were supposed to be praising, beyond the fact that he had lasted so long.[5]

In one of his many attacks on Menzies, Labor Prime Minster Keating agreed with Horne. "When Menzies retired," said Keating, "leader writers around the country found it difficult to find anything more than his political and oratorical skills to praise"[6]. Keating went further. It was not just that Menzies did nothing, but more importantly he left a poor policy legacy for Australia in terms of its protectionist import substitution industry policy that was unsuitable in the face of changed international economic circumstances that emerged in the mid-1970s. Menzies, thus "failed Australia" and "what Menzies called 'stability' ... really meant torpor and neglect".[7] On another occasion Keating attacked the Menzies era as the "lazy days of the 1950s and 1960s when policy could be adjusted at the margin ... decades of wasted opportunities".[8] Later Keating condemned Menzies' war leadership, his personal behaviour dredging up the pathetic attack on Menzies made in 1939 by Country Party leader Dr Earle Page and that he was a "woeful coward".[9] That Keating returned to attack Menzies so often, unprecedented in the practice of prime ministers concerning their predecessors, suggests how significant Menzies was in Australian history especially in keeping Labor out of office, and therefore how important it has been to besmirch Menzies' achievements, and therefore to rewrite history.

Although acknowledged that "the 1950s and 1960s were the 'golden age' of Australian economic growth"[10] critics like Judith Brett and others, believed "Menzies can take little direct credit for this" as "he showed little interest in economics".[11] Rather, the unprecedented period of low unemployment and economic growth was the result of the post World War Two international economic boom and iconic projects like the Snowy Mountains Scheme and the post war immigration program initiated by Labor governments and its embrace, like most other western countries, of Keynesian economics. This view largely persists. Even Troy Bramston, who is generally admiring in his portrayal of Menzies, especially of his political skills, style and principles, does not depart from this script. As he says:

> He (Menzies) <u>governed</u> (this author's emphasis) during a period of strong economic growth, low unemployment, increasing wages, rising living standards, and an expanding home-owning middle class. It was the 'golden age' of prosperity and stability, and a continuation of the post war nation-building ethos.[12]

The implications are clear – Menzies just happened to be in office during the good times. It was all so easy. There were few real challenges. He coasted and so did Australia. Such views are made with the benefits of hindsight and from very different perspectives and circumstances from the Menzies era.

Concerning social policy Dr Gwen Gray concluded that "the Menzies period can be seen as an area of modest action or incremental change when compared with activity in other countries or with activity in Australia in the periods before or after the long interval of Liberal-Country Party government".[13] The complaint was that Australian welfare expenditure only "grew slowly in the 1950s and 1960s" compared to OECD countries, causing the "underdevelopment of the Australian welfare state".[14]

In foreign affairs Keating argued that because of his anglophile bias Menzies "could never appreciate that our destiny was linked irrevocably with Asia,"[15] had no achievements, and worse was respected by no overseas leaders – Asian or otherwise.

Although it is acknowledged that Menzies' personal

interest in education drove the considerable expansion of higher education, these achievements have often been overshadowed and devalued by the Whitlam Labor Government's initiatives nearly two decades later.[16] Whitlam himself was less than impressed when in parliamentary debate in 1965 he observed:

> There is a sedulously fostered legend that education will be the Menzies Government's greatest monument. It could not possibly have done less than it has done.[17]

Although possibly excusable as reflecting the partisanship of an adversarial parliamentary debate, nevertheless, said Professor Reid of the University of Western Sydney, even "Whitlam would have known this assertion was far from the truth".[18] Nevertheless, Whitlam's own book 20 years later underrates Menzies' education achievements and overrates his own.[19]

Even Menzies' extension of Commonwealth funding to schools especially, but not only to the non-government sector, is condemned. This began the ending of the long running 'state-aid' debate in Australia.[20] It also meant the Commonwealth was at last providing additional support for all schools. It reflected a major new policy initiative based on principles of providing parents with choice and giving support to every child. Nevertheless, it has been portrayed as just a cynical exercise to buy Democratic Labor Party support[21] and as "reversing national policy ... a hundred years."[22]

Dr Graeme Starr labels these views as the "wasted years" argument whereby according to these critics nothing of substance was achieved during the Menzies period in office which was merely an "interregnum between the eras of Chifley and Whitlam".[23] Underpinning this has been the long pervading academic narrative of Australian political history that Labor was the party of initiative and reform and the non-Labor parties that of resistance and reaction. This was "an assertion frequently taken for granted" [24] and although seriously challenged and debunked by Henry Mayer[25] still permeates much of the discussion about Australian politics and Menzies.

There were other criticisms. Humphrey McQueen, even questioned Menzies' loyalty to Australia:

> He switched from British sycophant to American lickspittle and back again, with such easy conscience that his followers discovered in his lack of principle a species of gracefulness. Given the opportunity he undoubtedly could have found the resources within himself to head a Vichy-style regime for the Japanese.[26]

Indeed, says McQueen, Menzies was so beholden to external foreign interests that without their support "he would never have been elected even to the Malvern Council".[27]

Horne after Menzies' death concluded that the basis of his success as a politician was "his shrewd 'peasant mentality'" and compared his theatrical skills to

President Sukarno, former dictator of Indonesia.[28]

There are many reasons for this distorted view of Menzies. John Carroll attributes it to the "leftist construction of Australian history".[29] Paddy McGuinness claimed that "Menzies has been subjected to ... the most sustained campaign of denigration and belittlement of any figure in our history".[30] Perhaps, but the lack of any serious critical study of Menzies until the 1990s did not help to set the record straight. While there were personal reminiscences by those who worked closely with Menzies[31] and observations from those in the press gallery,[32] none provided the detailed analysis that Menzies and his long term in office deserved. "It is extraordinary," exclaimed journalist Michelle Grattan in 1988, "that a decade after his death, there is still no comprehensive definitive biography of Australia's longest serving prime minister".[33] In fairness, part of the problem was that Menzies' official biographer, Lady Frances McNicoll was given the task of preparing an official biography and had sole access to Menzies' private papers as early as 1972, never delivered. This had become evident by 1991.[34] Fortunately, Troy Bramston's recent study of Menzies salvaged some of McNicoll's work, thus providing insights that would otherwise have been lost.[35] That Menzies himself, unlike some recent former prime ministers, eschewed publishing a detailed defensive 'tell-all' personal history hardly help set the record straight. As he said in the first volume of his memoirs:

This is not a history ... I am not an historian. This
is a book of personal memories. It is not an essay
in self-justification; such things are wearisome, and
frequently distorted by personal bias.[36]

So, it was not until Dr Allan Martin's now highly
regarded[37] two volume biography of Menzies[38] released
in 1993 – some 15 years after Menzies' death in 1978,
and 27 years after his retirement in 1966, that a more
thorough portrayal of Menzies finally emerged.

Dr Graeme Starr provides another explanation for
the neglect of Menzies. He believes the Liberal Party
itself must take some responsibility. The problem, says
Starr, has been the Liberal Party's "failure ... to grasp
the importance of their own history" doing "little
to promote the memory or an image of Menzies,
even to their own members" and thus often leaving
Menzies' contributions to be defined "by those more
sympathetic to their opponents".[39] Others agree.[40]
By contrast, says Starr, the Labor Party turned their
vanquished leaders, like Chifley, Evatt, Calwell, and
most of all Whitlam, into revered heroes, exaggerating
their importance and contributions to the nation and
so camouflaging their personal flaws, electoral failures,
unpopularity, ineptness, policy mistakes and frequent
overreach. That it was not until 1994 that the Liberal
Party finally established the Menzies Research Centre
to be both a policy think tank and to rescue the party's
own history underlines this issue. "While the Liberals
still use Menzies' imagery," said one young academic

relatively recently on discovering his achievements, "they rarely do him justice".[41]

Consequently, it is unsurprising given the pervasiveness of these negative assessments that "if you're under 50 … chances are you heard little that was positive about Menzies".[42] Unsurprising that evaluations of Australian prime ministers have never placed Menzies at the top. Abjorensen's 1992 study for the *Canberra Times*[43] rated Menzies fifth. The 2001 *Australian Financial Review*[44] and 2004 *Age* reviews[45] gave him second billing. The 2010 Monash University survey of a small number of politics academics[46] put Menzies fifth overall. Professor Pat Weller[47] drew attention that six of the Monash's eight leading prime ministers were Labor which was surprising given "Labor has governed in Australia for just over 30 per cent of the time since federation".[48] Further, notes Weller three of the six nominated Labor prime ministers led their parties to "devastating defeats that left the party out of office for years"[49] while another lost the leadership. Clearly, says Weller "the academic panel had different views from the Australian electorate about what prime ministers should do; perhaps the former ranked change and vision above management and stability and the electorate were content with the latter".[50] More pointedly, he noted that such surveys, "tell us more about the respondents than about the prime ministers".[51] Indeed!

So, there you have it. According to the conventional wisdom Menzies believed in nothing, his governments did nothing original, and held Australia back. They were the "wasted years" of Australian politics. The difficulties and challenges of the times are ignored, any achievements overlooked and Menzies' skills, including his electoral successes, downplayed.

Overview – the Menzies story[52]

Early life – the scholarship boy

Robert Gordon Menzies was born in 1894 in Jeparit in country Victoria – about 300 kilometres north of Melbourne. This date is important as its puts Menzies and his upbringing at a very particular time in history. He was the third son. His family were originally from Scotland. His father was a Methodist, but Menzies and his wife, Pattie, were Presbyterian all their lives. The Menzies were not a wealthy family but owned a small country store. They later moved to Melbourne. Indeed, Menzies was a scholarship boy – winning a scholarship first to Grenville College, Ballarat, and then to Wesley College Melbourne. He won another scholarship to enter the Law School at the University of Melbourne where he was an outstanding student winning numerous academic prizes. Menzies summed up his humble background in his first broadcast to the nation on becoming prime minister in 1939:

> I am a singularly plain man, born in the little town of Jeparit on the fringe of the Mallee; educated at Ballarat, in a State school, and then by scholarship

at a public school and Melbourne University. Apart
from having parents of great character, intelligence
and fortitude, I was not born to the purple.[53]

Menzies, unlike many of his ilk, such as Nationalist
Prime Minister Stanley Bruce (1923-29) and his later
rival, Richard Casey who were both educated in
England, did not seek to top up his education with a
stint at Oxford or Cambridge. Menzies did not visit
Britain till 1935 when he was 41 years old and that was
for official business.[54] Nor did Menzies speak with a
fabricated English upper class plummy accent as many
did on the non-Labor side of politics at that time. As
political scientist Don Rawson pointed out:

Menzies, was unmistakably an Australian type ...
His voice, with its well articulated consonants and
full vowels, could nevertheless be the product of no
other country other than his own ...[55]

Menzies' biographer, Dr Allan Martin observed,
that although Menzies always felt British in Britain,
"English journalists persisted in seeing him as an
archetypal Australian".[56]

Successful lawyer

Menzies was admitted to the bar in 1918 and soon
had a thriving law practice. He was articulate,
energetic and his participation in the pivotal High
Court *Engineer's Case* in 1920 at the age of 26 which
overturned precedent and expanded Commonwealth

powers, is testimony to his legal competencies. By way of interest the junior for the other side was his later Labor arch-rival, Herbert Vere Evatt (known as Bert).[57] His practice expanded. He was involved in many other High Court cases. Menzies was made a King's Counsel (KC) in 1929 – at just 35 years of age – the youngest in the nation and just beating Evatt by a few months. Menzies was reported as being Australia's highest paid KC. He could have continued in the law and enjoyed a very prosperous career.

On the domestic front Menzies married Pattie Maie Leckie in 1920 who came from Alexandra in northern Victoria and was educated in Melbourne. Pattie came from a political family. Her father, John Leckie was a non-Labor state and later federal parliamentarian and minister. Pattie gave strong support to Menzies throughout his long career, offering "her husband down-to-earth advice" and served "as a sounding board or, when necessary, a debunker".[58] Pattie also took an active interest in a wide range of charity activities. The Menzies had three children – two sons and a daughter.

Entering state parliament

Despite his success at law, politics soon beckoned Menzies. His family background and marriage encouraged this while the legal profession lent itself to this path, but it was more than this. Menzies had a genuine desire to make a contribution and he had a lot to offer. As he said later about the attraction of politics:

> In the daily life of the plain citizen there is scarcely one hour or one activity which is unaffected by what politicians in Congress or Parliament determine ... That ... is why I believe that politics is the most important and responsible civil activity to which a man may devote his character, his talents, and his energy.[59]

In 1928 Menzies entered Victoria's upper house and was made an Honorary Minister (minister without portfolio) in the new Nationalist Party government. The following year he moved to the Legislative Assembly winning the seat of Nunawading at the state election that brought Labor to office. In 1932 with the fall of the Labor government, Menzies became Attorney-General and Minister for Railways in the new government. He also became Deputy Premier. His reputation as a brilliant speaker and effective minister was quickly established.

Entering Commonwealth parliament and the ministry

Menzies' horizons were broader than Victoria. He was responsible with others in forming the new United Australia Party (UAP) that would absorb the previous Nationalist Party. Menzies helped persuade Joseph Lyons, a disillusioned federal Labor frontbencher, who was also acting Treasurer[60] in the Scullin Labor Government (1929-1932), to defect and become the leader of the UAP. The UAP's more conventional and moderate response to the Great Depression appealed to Lyons who was alarmed at the unorthodox expansionary proposals by federal Labor Treasurer E.G. Theodore and the radical views by New South Wales Labor premier Jack Lang who wanted to renege on overseas loans. Lyons defected, became leader of the UAP and in coalition with the Country Party led by Dr Earle Page, won the December 1931 federal election and thus became prime minister. He was to win two more elections in 1934 and 1937.

In 1934, Menzies, encouraged by Lyons, stood successfully as a UAP candidate for the seat of Kooyong and entered federal politics. He held this seat until retirement 32 years later. Menzies' abilities and reputation were recognised and he was almost immediately made Commonwealth Attorney General and Minister for Industry and deputy UAP leader. Menzies quickly made his mark as a key member of the Lyons Government, but his brusque manner and air of superiority alienated many in the government. In cabinet it was reported that his behaviour antagonised, among others, the Country Party leader Earle Page, and upset an ailing Lyons. Don Whitington, perhaps not always sympathetic to Menzies, wrote:

> Cabinet meetings were a farce ... Menzies criticised, obstructed, mischievously mocked and generally made merry. Lyons was frustrated and bewildered; the Country Party, butt of most of Menzies' barbed

shafts, was furiously impotent. Only the Attorney
General (Menzies) emerged from Cabinet smiling.[61]

Menzies' temporary resignation from cabinet in March 1939 over the Lyons Government's decision not to proceed with a national health insurance scheme, although applauded as an act of principle, was also seen by some as the ambitious Menzies seeking to undermine Lyons so as to become prime minister. Dame Enid Lyons, the prime minister's wife, and herself later a federal parliamentarian summed up Menzies' actions observing that:

> For Menzies it was a continuing clash between desire and loyalty: the desire of a young ambitious man convinced of his own power to serve his country well, and the loyalty he owed to the Leader who had given years of selfless service, but whose capacity for further leadership he genuinely doubted. [62]

Becoming prime minister 1939

The leadership issue was resolved, though not immediately, by Lyons' sudden death in early April 1939 – a month after Menzies' resignation. Page became acting prime minister until the UAP, as the larger party, elected a new leader. At that juncture Page, a target of Menzies' slights, stated he would refuse to serve in cabinet if Menzies became the new UAP leader. Fellow Country Party members agreed and passed a resolution that it was "definitely unable to co-operate with the Hon R.G. Menzies KC as its prime minister".[63] Attempts by

Page and some UAP members such as Casey to recruit former Nationalist prime minister Stanley Bruce, then Australian High Commissioner in London, to the vacant position failed. Despite Page's threats, the UAP elected Menzies as leader by a slender four vote margin, but he was still not yet prime minister. Before tendering his commission to the Governor-General, Page made a scathing denunciation in parliament about Menzies' alleged lack of service in World War One. Menzies was undeterred, rebuffed the allegations and became prime minister a few days later. However, the Country Party remained out of the government so, for a time, Menzies led a minority government juggling both the Labor opposition and the renegade Country Party. It was another challenge to his talents.

As Menzies later reflected, he had "enjoyed a very rapid rise to the top position"[64] from state politician to prime minister, but it had certainly not been without many personal and political hurdles. His resilience and staying power are worth noting. It will become even more important later in his career at many junctures. Now in office he faced further challenges. In September, Australia joined Britain and other allies and entered into what was to become World War Two. It was Menzies who announced that it was his "melancholy duty to inform you officially that, in consequence of a persistence by Germany in her invasion of Poland, Great Britain has declared war on her, and that, as a result, Australia is also at war".[65] The Menzies Government thus had the daunting task of putting Australia on a full war footing and galvanising public support. The Labor Opposition refused to join a national government as happened in Britain. During 1940 a plane accident in Canberra in August 1940 meant Menzies lost three of his ablest ministers and closest supporters. The federal election was due in December that year, but as the accident would have necessitated three by-elections it was brought forward to 21 September. The Government, now again joined by the Country Party following the replacement of Page as leader, performed poorly at the September 1940 election, but retained office as a minority government. Menzies was confronted by continual internal party intrigues and criticisms over the war effort especially in relation to standing up to Britain concerning Australia's regional anxieties and the deployment of Australian troops in the Middle East. That Labor was becoming a more potent political force under John Curtin was another pressure. Further offers to Labor to form a national government were all rejected.

Finally, after returning from a four month official visit to the Middle East and Great Britain in early 1941, that included visits to Australian troops, meetings with the British War Cabinet, and arguments with Churchill over Australia's defence needs,[66] Menzies faced a hostile party room and resigned the prime ministership. In his place the coalition parties elected Country Party leader Arthur Fadden as the new prime minister, although Menzies remained leader of the UAP. Fadden did not last long – just 40 days with the government falling on a vote of confidence bringing Labor to power. At the subsequent coalition meeting, the UAP, although the major coalition party, opted for Fadden to be the Opposition Leader. It is at this point that Menzies stepped down as leader of the UAP and retired to the backbench for two years commenting that "a party of our numbers which is not prepared to lead is not worth leading".[67] Meanwhile, the UAP limped on under the leadership of the 79 year old former Labor and Nationalist prime minister, Billy Hughes, until it was decimated at the 1943 Labor landslide election. It seemed that Menzies and the non-Labor cause was finished. Billy Hughes declared at the time, Menzies "couldn't lead a flock of homing pigeons".[68]

Menzies' first term as prime minister was seen a failure in terms of his leadership style, his electoral appeal and his achievements as war prime minister. There has also been the criticism that Menzies was an appeaser of Hitler prior to the outbreak of hostilities. So could Lyons and others be so described. However, it is now agreed that this was very much in line with most at the time. Few prior to 1939 had the prescience of Australian academic Professor Stephen Roberts[69] or previously side-lined House of Commons backbencher, Winston Churchill, about the forthcoming threat from Nazi Germany.[70] It is now recognised that the Menzies Government made considerable progress in preparing Australia for war and that Australia's interests were strongly presented by Menzies to the British Government, though it was not made public at the time.[71] Perhaps more importantly was what his failure at this time taught Menzies about himself, working with others and governing. The lessons, if learnt, would be vital if Menzies were to stay in politics. Hasluck explained the failure of Menzies' first prime ministership very much in terms of his grating personality, style and manner:

> He came to the prime ministership at a time when his great gifts of advocacy, logical exposition of his lofty concept of Liberal principles, his knowledge of the law, and the world and his professional competence were to count less than the shrewdness, human understanding and skill in political management that keeps difficult people working together, the human ordinariness that does not invite enmity or expose itself to attack, the administrative training and experience which ensures that each decision leads to effective action …[72]

Menzies himself accepted that his personal style had alienated many in his party and its coalition partner the Country Party and that he "had to acquire the common touch". [73]. Retiring to the backbench he later observed, "did me personally a lot of good".[74] Learning from his mistakes was, as journalist Paul Kelly and others were to observe later, was one of Menzies' great attributes which would contribute to his more successful second term as prime minister.[75]

A new beginning and founding the Liberal Party

Indeed, Menzies may have been on the backbench, but he was not idle. In 1942 he began his "Forgotten People" radio broadcasts which in time would become the basis for a new philosophy for the revived non-Labor side of politics. Following the disastrous 1943 election Menzies became leader of the UAP again and leader of the Opposition. However, he saw that the UAP was finished, and believed there was a need for a completely new non-Labor political force if Labor was to be successfully challenged. In 1944 Menzies and others organised two major meetings that brought together the many disparate parts of the non-Labor side of politics to form a new political party. This became the Liberal Party – a name Menzies deliberately chose to reflect that the new party was to be a "progressive party, willing to make experiments, in no sense reactionary".[76] The Country Party was not invited and continued to develop as a separate party. Menzies became the new party's first leader. No-one else was in serious contention. And there is little doubt that the new party was, as Gerard Henderson put it, "Menzies' Child".[77] However, there were doubts that given the past faltering record of non-Labor parties that the Liberal Party would last or that Menzies would ever lead it to victory. The conventional wisdom at this point was "You can't win with Menzies".[78]

More disappointments

It was not plain sailing under the new Liberal banner. Its first test, the 1946 election, was disappointing with Labor easily retaining office under their new leader Ben Chifley who had become prime minister following Curtin's death a year earlier. The conventional wisdom about Menzies electability seemed correct. Menzies' position as leader after the election was far from secure, but again he pressed on. His professionalism and commitment to developing a real alternative to Labor and its agenda is seen in how he used this time in opposition. He could have returned full time to the bar. Instead, he put his time and energy into studying international developments in politics, campaign techniques and trends in the mass media. He dabbled in journalism for the *London Times* and *New York Times Magazine*. His appreciation of the value of the radio medium in politics had already been shown by the aforementioned "Forgotten People" broadcasts.[79] It was a skill he would use to good effect in the run-up to the next election. Between 1946 and 1949 he travelled frequently to the United Kingdom, and the United States giving particular attention to trends in the news media and modern communications including television which he predicted would "sweep the world before too long".[80] In 1948 he spent time in America covering the presidential election for the Melbourne *Herald*. Menzies was developing an understanding of modern communications and the art of conveying complex messages that voters understood.

Prime minister the second time and retirement

All this paid off. Finally, in December 1949 Menzies led the Liberal Party to victory – not a landslide, but a secure one. Menzies was prime minister again. He went on to win six more elections (1951, 1954, 1955, 1958, 1961 and 1963), though unexpectedly almost losing in 1961. He retired in January 1966. Knighted in 1963, Menzies was chosen by the British Government as Churchill's successor to the honorary post of Lord Warden of the Cinque Ports. He soon published his highly regarded work on the operations of the federal system and the growth of Commonwealth power[81] making accurate predictions about how this would continue to accrue. Two volumes of memoirs followed[82] along with other essays, and lectures including at important international forums. With a few exceptions he rarely made public comments on current politics.[83] Menzies died in 1978 aged 84. All Australia mourned.

What Menzies did

Given the conventional wisdom that Menzies achieved little except 'preside' over events during his sixteen years in office, assessing what he did should be brief. On the contrary, in reviewing the challenges Menzies faced, the numerous elections he fought and won, his many initiatives, and his very style of leadership and government, there is so much to cover. So, the coverage had to be selective. Certainly, some of the major policy areas like the economy, social welfare, housing and education are given prime attention. Foreign affairs is also considered given its particular salience during this period with the 'Cold War' and its impact on domestic politics.

While policies are important, effective government is more than just making announcements and launching numerous initiatives. It also involves setting priorities, appreciating the limits of a government's capabilities, and in a federal system, appreciating what a national government can and cannot do. It is about establishing the administrative processes to ensure policies are implemented and knowing how to pace change so that institutions do not become overloaded and the electorate can have time to understand, absorb and support new policies. All this requires skills in gaining the electorate's confidence, what Menzies called in his 1948 *New York Times* article[84] and later published work, "the art of politics" which he defined as being:

> ... to convey ideas to others, if possible to persuade a majority to agree, to create or encourage a public opinion so soundly that it endures, and is not blown aside by chance winds; to persuade people to take long-range views.[85]

This was one of Menzies great attributes which Troy Bramston has given particular attention to in his recent biography.[86] It is one of the important contributions he makes in providing a better appreciation of Menzies' abilities.

Consequently, attention is given in this monograph to

how Menzies governed, in particular to how he shaped executive government, managed the public service, worked through the federal system, and timed and paced policy change. In addition, consideration is also given to how Menzies maintained such exceptional cordiality with his Country Party coalition partner over sixteen years. Its success was fundamental to the order and stability which marked his long second term in office.

In this assessment four issues are considered. First, did the policies pursued by Menzies and his governments reflect any of the principles and philosophy on which the new Liberal Party had been founded or were they just governments driven by short-term pragmatism and political opportunism? Second, given that Menzies was supposed to owe so much of his success to the policies inherited from Labor, were there any divergences from these and if Labor had been in office would its policies have been the same? Third, was it all 'so easy' both politically and economically for Menzies requiring few difficult decisions or challenges? Last, were these really the 'wasted years,' were there any major 'missed opportunities,' and if so, what were they?

Clarifying Menzies' principles

Although Menzies and the Liberal Party were, in keeping with Australian politics generally, pragmatic, it would be misleading to assume his governments were without principles or any overarching philosophy. Indeed, in establishing the Liberal Party in 1944 Menzies was anxious to avoid the flaws of its predecessors – organisationally, politically, and especially in policy terms concerning the role of government. Menzies, as a former war prime minister, understood the increasing necessary role of government not just in wartime situations, but into the future if unemployment was to be avoided and economic prosperity sustained. He appreciated and embraced wholeheartedly the new Keynesian ideas to manage the economy and the prime importance of keeping unemployment down. He identified the flaws of the Liberal Party's predecessors of "appearing to resist economic and political progress ... to be branded as reactionaries ... unduly satisfied with our existing state of affairs".[87] By contrast, Menzies believed "there is no room for a party of reaction. There is no useful place for a policy of negation".[88] Menzies believed his governments "have not just kept the ring and allowed victory to go to the strong,"[89] but rather "where government action or control has seemed to us to be the best answer to a practical problem, we have adopted that answer".[90] Nevertheless, said Menzies, "our first impulse is always to seek the private enterprise answer, to help the individual help himself, to create a climate, economic, social, industrial favourable to his activity and growth".[91] Assessing how Menzies managed this approach will be considered.

Understanding context

Of course, how a government governs, the choices
it makes and the risks it is prepared to take will be
determined by its hold on power including: the size of
its majorities; control of the Senate; and what has been
called its 'political capital'.[92] In addition, all governments
are buffeted by unexpected factors over which they
have limited control. The post war period over which
Menzies governed has been too easily labelled as one
of untrammelled economic growth posing few policy
challenges to incumbent governments – the only
decisions that had to be made were, as Mr Keating
reminded us, just "at the margin." Later governments
and leaders have an interest in wanting to recast the
past as being an easier time than their own to inflate
their own challenges and achievements. Perhaps, this
is another explanation of why Menzies has been so
belittled in recent times.

On the contrary, as highlighted, the Menzies period
was more complex than has been portrayed when
"appearances often belied reality and masked
considerable change".[93] There were many challenges
– economically, socially, and internationally.
Economically, the world was entering the post-
war era with new international financial and trade
arrangements. Socially, Australia was embarking on
a massive immigration program that would bring 2.5
million people to the country from a more diverse
range of nations than previously.[94] It was the beginning

of multicultural Australia. Internationally, much was in flux and accompanied with real dangers that were not limited to distant Europe. There were real Cold War tensions between the West and the USSR and the emerging Communist China and the threat of nuclear war. A further factor creating instability and uncertainty was the process of decolonialisation for many European countries, and most relevant for Australia and Menzies, was the disassembling of the British Empire and Britain's diminution as a world power and its retreat to Europe. The "winds of change" as British Prime Minister Harold Macmillan[95] described this process, was just beginning and was to blow ever stronger during Menzies' term.

Much could go wrong.

Election wins were not so easy

Menzies' political ascendancy and seven election wins have been portrayed as being easy, predictable, aided by uninterrupted economic growth, a disunited opposition, international tensions and security fears, and a biased electoral system.[96] Menzies' election record has been considered in more detail by others[97] suffice to highlight that nothing was certain, predictable and or inevitable about his seven election wins. His now perceived political ascendency was neither immediate nor apparent at the time.

Menzies first three elections – 1949, 1951 and 1954,

were, with the exception of his initial 1949 win, not predictable. That they were all fought on the electoral redistribution passed by Labor in 1948 removes the validity of the criticism that Menzies only won because of a biased electoral system.[98] Despite his strong win in 1949 Menzies did not gain control of the Senate thanks to changes made by Labor a year before in changing the voting system and enlarging the size of the Senate to deliberately thwart an expected Liberal win.

Menzies went early in 1951 and called a double dissolution to gain control of the Senate. It was a great risk. The only previous double dissolution (1914) had resulted in the government concerned losing office. There were economic problems caused by the Korean war (1950-53). Menzies won, but with a reduced majority, though he gained control of the Senate. However, Menzies' constitutional referendum held later that year to ban the Communist Party, despite polls to the contrary, failed. Menzies was out-campaigned by new Labor leader Bert Evatt.

The May 1954 election was made against the backdrop of the Petrov Soviet spy defection, a subsequent royal commission, and a slowing economy. Labor won five extra seats and 50 per cent of the total vote, but not office. It was close. Conspiracy theories that the Petrov affair had all been concocted by Menzies and that the defection yielded no intelligence value to the West[99] have been subsequently proved groundless by scholars.[100] Furthermore, the election was not solely about the Petrov issue. As one historian concluded:

> In the campaign ... the press and the Country Party
> capitalised on the Petrov affair, but the Liberals
> in general, and Menzies in particular, stood on
> their record and were very effective scorning of
> Evatt's platform of generous welfare pledges,
> including abolition of the means test for pension
> qualification.[101]

Only with the 1955 election when government received
a swing of 4.7 per cent and won eleven seats did
Menzies' political ascendancy really begin. Remember,
this was nearly six years after Menzies had first won
office. The election had been called early to capitalise
on Evatt's inept responses[102] to the just released report
of the Petrov Royal Commission[103] and the emerging
Labor split.

This success was solidified in 1958 with further gains
which "put the Coalition Government in a seemingly
impregnable position".[104] In reality, this was short-
lived. Unexpectedly, Menzies only just won the 1961
election by one seat highlighting the precariousness of
office for any government. Menzies held on, exerted
control, made policy changes, and called an early 1963
election, and picked up ten seats. It was his last election.
He left a sound foundation for his successor, Harold
Holt, who went on to score the Coalition's then biggest
win at that time at the November 1966 election. As
Menzies said when he phoned Holt from Virginia,
United States, "You've done better without me."

In summary, Menzies' electoral successes were not certain. It reflected his skills and what Menzies called the "art of politics". He was a good campaigner and understood modern communications. His electoral meetings given his skills in interacting with audiences "became an evening out".[105] Also, he took risks – going early in 1951, 1955 and 1963. He exploited his adversary's weaknesses ruthlessly and he understood the electorate. He also understood the election machinery for as Mackerras points out, "Menzies is unique among Australian prime ministers in that he campaigned in all four types of election"[106] that were available.

And to clarify, Menzies and the coalition did not win because this was a period of political apathy, lack of participation, or limited debate. On the contrary, it was when political parties had their biggest memberships, elected members were most in contact with their communities, grassroots campaigning extensive, public rallies well attended, voting levels high, and issues and elections hotly contested.

Menzies' economic miracle?

The key issue concerning the Menzies era, acknowledged as the "golden age of Australian economic growth"[107] is whether it was a foregone conclusion, easily achieved, requiring no difficult decisions, and driven by the post war international boom, and the policies laid down by Menzies' immediate predecessor – the Chifley Labor

Government (1945-49). Indeed, were the economic policies pursued by Menzies really reflective of the Liberal Party's philosophy and distinct from Labor's?

Despite what Keating and others say, managing the economy during this period was not easy or straightforward. There was fear of a return to 1930s levels of mass unemployment, trepidation that over-reliance on rural exports would lead to a boom-bust economy, disruptions caused by the Korean War, concerns about changing trade patterns, new international agreements, balance of payments and foreign investment issues, and industrial relations problems in some areas. Who said managing the economy was ever easy?

Certainly, the previous Labor administration had laid some groundwork for future economic prosperity with its 1945 *White Paper on Full Employment*, adoption of Keynesian economics and establishment of the Post War Reconstruction Department and policies. There were also its iconic projects like the Snowy Mountain Hydro-Electric Scheme and the expanded immigration program. But let's be clear. Labor was in power for only just over three years after the war. These new policies were just being announced and had yet to be fully operationalised[108] and to face the normal vicissitudes of politics, changing international economic circumstances and unexpected events. Some of these new policy ideas had hardly been tried in normal peacetime situations. While the new immigration policy was underway by 1949, others. like the Snowy Scheme, was in its infancy.[109] By contrast, the Menzies Government was in power for 16 years. So, although Menzies adopted some of Labor's key planks, it had the more onerous task of having to make them work, adapting them when needed, and developing new policies to meet other emerging issues.

In summary, the economic and social policies pursued by the Menzies Government involved: a strong commitment to full employment; Keynesian anti-cyclical demand management; arbitrated wages through a regulated industrial relations system; tariff protection to allow a broad range of industrial development, especially manufacturing; housing and financial policies to give many access to and full ownership by the time most people retired; and strict means testing and targeting for most welfare incomes that was financed mainly by a progressive income tax.

While these policies reflected the overwhelming consensus of economic advice at the time, and to which Labor would largely agree concerning its core elements, there were differences. For instance, the Menzies Government had clearly departed from some of Labor's more direct interventionist policies like nationalisation which remained Labor's preferred approach as it was with Labour in the United Kingdom. The Menzies Government ran a comparatively tighter fiscal policy than many overseas countries or what it would have been under Labor especially given Evatt's

1954 election promises spending spree and Labor's budget responses.[110] Australia avoided the unfunded welfare policies of European systems and thus caused less demand on national savings. There was an upward moderate movement in government spending, but it stabilised from 1953-1964 at 18-19 per cent of GDP. Foreign investment was welcomed and fuelled considerable economic development, but was opposed by Labor. So too, was the pivotal 1957 *Australia-Japan Agreement on Commerce* "unwisely opposed" by Evatt.[111] The immigration program was maintained throughout the period, and although Menzies always gave credit to its originator, Arthur Calwell, Immigration Minister in the Chifley Government,[112] it was modified and extended to a wider range of groups.[113] Oddly, Labor criticised the immigration program when there were slight increases in unemployment or when housing shortages occurred. The Menzies Government's moves to establish the Reserve Bank of Australia in 1960 regarded as "a fundamental turning point in the history of central banking in Australia"[114] was resisted by Labor. Indeed, Menzies' earlier legislation to improve the operations of the Commonwealth Bank had been blocked by Labor in the Senate in 1951. It was one of the triggers for the 1951 double dissolution election.

A striking example of the differences between Liberals and Labor concerning microeconomic policy can be seen in relation to the airlines. Labor unsuccessfully attempted to nationalise the airlines in 1947 and to create a single government airline monopoly. Philosophically, the Liberals opposed this – having a single government monopoly meant no choice, no competition, and no private enterprise. In office, the Liberals retained the government airline, but through regulation (capacity control, parallel flight times, and import controls on planes) ensured that a private operator (eventually Ansett) could compete on equal terms with the government one – hence the 'two airline policy.' In an industry which economists regarded as a natural oligopoly with limited opportunities for unrestricted competition anyway, it was a sensible compromise and "represented a break towards a significantly more pro-competition and pro-private enterprise approach".[115] The policy was to remain till the 1980s and while the current deregulatory regime delivers cheaper airfares, industry instability remains.

On some areas of economic policy Menzies, for a person, as suggested by Brett, allegedly not interested in economics, took a surprising lead, albeit with strong Treasury advice. His scuttling of the Vernon Committee of Economic Enquiry is a case in point. Established in 1962 largely at the behest of his powerful Minister for Trade and Industry, Jack McEwen, leader of the Country Party and Deputy Prime Minister, the Vernon Report proposed increased government intervention and an Advisory Council on Economic Growth. It was a move to indicative economic planning in vogue overseas. Menzies (and Treasury), opposed it on economic, political and administrative grounds.

Politically, such a council might exercise too much pressure on government to pursue certain policies. Economically, its more interventionist approach was seen as inimical to Australia's long-term interests. Administratively, such a council was a potential competitor to Treasury in providing economic advice. Whatever the merits or otherwise of the Vernon Report's recommendations, Menzies shredded it in a skilful parliamentary performance.[116] McEwen, its real advocate, had to sit and nod in agreement. Menzies was in charge. While some mourned this as a 'missed opportunity,' others believe Menzies "should be congratulated"[117] for saving Australia from wasted bureaucratic effort and inappropriate government intervention.

Overall, then how do we view the Menzies Government's management of the Australian economy over these 16 years? There is no doubt Australia enjoyed an unprecedented period of high economic growth, low unemployment, low interest rates, rising real incomes and low inflation (most of the time). Home ownership reached record levels (see below). Was this success merely an extension of Labor's program laid down between 1945-49 with a few embellishments? Was it only the result of the international post war boom? Many other countries also enjoyed these opportunities, but not all availed themselves of it as well as Australia. Success was not automatic. Australia was able to benefit during these times because the decision makers in the Menzies Government in both political and public service offices, supported the new international changes and agreements and leveraged off these to Australia's advantage. Australia's economic performance was not just a by-product of good economic management "at the margin," or the result of a couple of iconic projects inherited from Labor. Rather, it reflected policies that were distinctive, and which the Menzies Government actively, constantly, and consciously strove for, year in, year out.

There were mistakes. The Menzies Government was slow in responding to inflationary pressures and applying the fiscal brake with its 1951-2 'horror' budget. It moved too fast and harshly in instigating the 1960 'credit squeeze.' Balance of payments crises which occurred several times were handled by harsh regulatory mechanisms like import controls. Tariff policy and 'all round protection' increased too much. Industrial relations remained highly regulated, but with 64 per cent of the workforce in trade unions was there an alternative? There was a reluctance to adopt more planning, but with a consistently growing economy it was not seen as being needed or desirable. As Geoffrey Bolton suggested the Australian electorate had grown "sceptical about the merits of planning; it seemed too often like interferences with the enjoyment of good things which were at last abundant".[118] Reliance on overseas investment did not come without some liabilities such as an over-dependency on overseas research and increased foreign ownership. Australia did slip down the international league table of growth per head, but this reflected other countries coming from a different base than any major shortfalls in Australian economic policy.

As to the Keating complaint that the Menzies' economic policies left Australia vulnerable in the 1980s, Ergas and Pincus conclude that while some of these "contributed to Australia's later difficulties"[119] (eg tariffs which became excessive and the regulated industrial relations system) "had Labor prevailed, the adjustment problems Australia faced in the 1970s and 1980s would have been more intractable and even more costly to resolve".[120]

Overall, despite some ad hoc and short-term decision making for which any government could be legitimately criticised,[121] the outcomes were probably better than if Labor had held full sway. Ergas and Pincus sum up the distinctions thus:

> ... the distinctive feature of the Menzies era – that differentiated it from the stance adopted by the Australian Labor Party and from the approach pursued in much of Europe and even more so in developing economies – was that its core beliefs were consciously implemented through policies which relied primarily on stimulating private initiative rather than replacing it ... The Menzies Government resisted the siren calls for nationalisation ... (and) indicative planning.[122]

As another historian concluded "by the beginning of the 1970s Australia enjoyed a fairly well balanced industrial economy"[123] or in the words of Professor Arndt, Australia had become a "small rich industrial country".[124] As to whether the Menzies Government's policies were responsible or not for this great success from 1949-1966 historian Geoffrey Bolton concludes that, "it would be stretching the arm of coincidence too far to assert that the government which held office for the whole of that period had nothing to do with this improvement".[125]

Finally, all this questions the view as to whether Australia could have been led by a prime minister as disinterested in economics as was alleged about Menzies. Dr H.C. Coombs, Governor of the Commonwealth Bank (1949-60) and then Governor of the Reserve Bank of Australia (1960-68) and an adviser to many governments made this assessment about Menzies:

> When there were economic problems of sufficient magnitude to demand his attention he would give it wholeheartedly ... he had an unusual capacity to grasp the essentials of the problem and to assess the action proposed.[126]

Social policy

In terms of social policy, the Menzies era was one when the modern welfare state as developed by the preceding Labor administration of 1941-49 and extended by the 1946 constitutional referendum – was confirmed, developed, and entrenched – not dismantled. The complaint, as noted by Gray earlier, was that it was not further extended by very much.

The remarkable achievement of the Menzies Government, for a government with a sometimes tenuous hold on power, was that there was no attempt to match the extravagant promises made by Labor to greatly extend social welfare especially at the 1954 election where Evatt promised so much.[127] For the Menzies Government, as Keating was to echo years later, the best welfare was full employment, a growing economy, low interest rates and price stability. Ergas and Pincus stress there was little debate about social policy or even taxation policy during this period because "in an era that saw economic growth and full employment as the primary means of meeting social aspirations, these were never rated as priorities".[128]

Again as in other areas, Menzies' social welfare policies were a mixture of principles stressing individual responsibility, supported by low unemployment, growing wages, and low inflation with pragmatic responses and incremental adjustments to meet immediate needs rather than to promote grandiose visions. There was for instance, steady liberalisation of the pensions means test. In 1947 37.5 per cent of age eligible persons received a pension. By 1966 this had increased to 52.9 per cent and by 1970 to 60.2 per cent. Social welfare during this period was designed to be a 'safety net' – which given the low unemployment levels was more than enough – and better than other places like United States. Menzies' social policies were in very much in the liberal tradition rather than a doctrinaire socialist one. They were not about affecting a society's direction – but more about responding to an individual's needs – a subtle, but important distinction.

Much has been made since about the lack of Commonwealth attention to Aborigines during this period. It should be remembered that throughout the Menzies period, Aborigines were not a Commonwealth constitutional responsibility – they were firmly under the jurisdiction of the states – sometimes Labor ones. This, of course excludes the Northern Territory that was a Commonwealth responsibility. Also, in Paul Hasluck as Minister for Territories for twelve years, Aborigines had a sympathetic and understanding voice in cabinet, but there was persistent resistance for additional Commonwealth funding to the states for Aborigines as was occurring gradually in other areas. There was progress. In 1959 the Menzies Government extended Aboriginal eligibility for social security benefits. Voting rights were extended quickly following the recommendations of the 1961 House of Representatives Select Committee on Voting Rights for Aborigines, though enrolment for Aborigines was not made compulsory till 1984. Also, although "somewhat belatedly"[129] it was Menzies who in 1965 announced that in response to the recommendations of a 1959 parliamentary committee[130] that there would be a constitutional referendum to delete Section 127 of the Constitution.[131] Menzies' retirement in January

1966, the succession of Harold Holt as prime minister, and the November 1966 general election delayed the referendum till 1967. It was overwhelmingly passed. Significantly, it included an additional change to Section 51 xxvi that had excluded the Commonwealth from making laws for Aborigines. This had not been a recommendation of the parliamentary committee, although representations about it had been made, but had not been accepted by the Menzies Government. Sanders' assessment of the Menzies period is that many of the issues now a legitimate part of this area were just not on the agenda at that time. His overall view is that the "Menzies Government's record in Aboriginal policy was one of action on equal rights, but inaction on a greater Commonwealth role".[132] Could the Menzies Government have done better? Possibly, but the constitutional constraints till the referendum passed were real and the political pressure for change were slight.

Women too, from today's perspective, seemed to have been neglected across a range of areas. Again, these issues were only just emerging on the policy agenda in the latter part of the Menzies period and both major parties took time to engage. However, any reading of Menzies' speeches in establishing the Liberal Party and in its policy platforms showed an awareness of providing support for women in terms of both 'traditional' family roles and those concerning careers and education.[133] The initial Liberal Party platform advocated "equality of opportunity, liberties and status

for men and women".[134] Menzies had no hesitation
to support women pursuing careers though today's
extensive arrangements were unthought of then.
With its special Women's Council and female vice-
presidents' positions, the Liberal Party was much more
organisationally structured to attract women, to hear
their views and to inform policy than the Labor Party.
This, along with the policies pursued around housing
and families, explains why the Liberal Party received a
far higher proportion of the female vote than Labor
during this period.[135]

In summing up, some believe that Menzies left
Australia with an underdeveloped welfare state making
it an international laggard in terms of spending and
range of policies. The alternative view is that the
Menzies' approach left Australia with a welfare system
that was highly targeted to those most in need and
economically sustainable. Economic commentator
Maximillian Walsh concluded that in relation to social
welfare policies, "Menzies was right after all." As Walsh
explains:

> The Menzies Government was not immune to the
> climate of welfarism which characterised the post-
> war years, but unlike the European governments, for
> instance, it was a reluctant redistributor of income.
> While some like myself – of course much younger
> then – regarded the Menzies Government as being
> out of touch with the role of a modern government,
> time has vindicated its conservative approach.[136]

Housing

It is worth highlighting Menzies' achievements in promoting home ownership. At one level it was an extension of social policy. However, it had wider cultural and political implications. Home ownership in Australia increased dramatically under Menzies from 53 per cent in 1947 to 70 per cent by 1961 and even further by 1970. This was higher than in the United Kingdom where ownership levels were 41 per cent in 1961 and more than in most European countries. This was not accidental. It was the result of deliberate policy that was also philosophically driven. As Menzies wrote in his "Forgotten People" address in 1942:

> The home is the foundation of sanity and sobriety;
> it is the indispensable condition of continuity; its
> health determines the health of society as a whole
> ... homes material, homes human, and homes
> spiritual.[137]

Menzies put an emphasis on private home ownership as the basis of creating a stable, thrifty, self-reliant and independent society firmly anchored in work and family responsibilities. Increased home ownership was not just a by-product of the full employment, rising real wages, and low interest rates that marked the period. That provided the means. Promoting home ownership was a clear policy imperative throughout the Menzies period. It was underpinned by real policy initiatives. For instance, the 1956 Commonwealth-State Housing Agreement (note the date) when allocating funds for the states to distribute was increasingly orientated to private home ownership rather than public housing. It was further buttressed by changes to the taxation system that provided deductions for dependents which, along with child endowment, gave further financial support for families and thus incentives for home ownership. At the 1963 election Menzies announced two further initiatives. One helped first home buyers bridge the deposit gap (The Home Savings Grant Scheme). The other, by establishing the National Housing Insurance Corporation allowed eligible purchasers to borrow a higher proportion of the value of a house than previously.[138]

Undoubtedly, Menzies' policy had political motivations. One was to have a distinct difference to Labor's approach. The other was to give support to whom Menzies had described as the "forgotten people" and garner their support.

Labor's policies, like its counterpart in the UK, "focussed upon the public provision" of housing "believing that private enterprise did not have the capacity to meet the shortfall"[139] in housing demands. It had little interest in promoting home ownership *per se*. Labor framed its housing policies in "abstract and functional terms"[140] such as the national interest and efficiencies in terms of numbers built, people accommodated and low costs. As John Dedman, Labor Minister for Post War Reconstruction said during the debates on the Commonwealth-State

Housing Agreement Bill in 1945 the "Commonwealth Government is concerned to provide adequate and good housing for the workers; it is not concerned with making the workers into little capitalists".[141]

By contrast Menzies stressed both material and emotional benefits around families and home ownership. Owner occupied housing gave workers a "stake in their nation" that "helped tie the social fabric together and promoted respect for private property".[142] It was an anchor of social stability. While Labor was providing an ideological response to housing needs – public housing and rented accommodation – Menzies' policies were meeting real electorate demands that had been enabled by increased prosperity. Menzies' policies helped create modern suburbia with houses on their individual blocks of land. Sneered at by some because of their individual design ('featurism') and location away from city centres,[143] but it was desired by most. It was in the Menzies era which saw this notion of individual self-help, family ties and pride in home ownership firmly established in the Australian psyche – what has been dubbed "home centred independent individualism".[144] Menzies' "politicisation of domesticity reached across the public-private divide, drawing on citizens' identities as mothers, fathers, lovers and spouses to create a political constituency".[145] The forgotten people said one observer "were now far from being forgotten"[146].

The perceived political impacts of Menzies' policies are best summarised in ANU academic L.F. Crisp's assessment. He concluded that Menzies' policies encouraged the movement of workers and families to the "newer, outer suburbs" where, lacking the inner city feelings of class solidarity, they tended to identify less with socialist policies and the Labor Party and thus were more willing to vote for an alternative – the Liberal Party.[147]

Menzies' great insight as seen in his housing policy was an appreciation that policy "should accord with the traditions and habits of society."[148] But Menzies did more than just reflect traditions of society. His government's active and successful pursuit of home ownership against the prevailing economic, social and planning orthodoxies of the time, created a new tradition, an Australian tradition, that still holds true in this country in the 21st Century.

Menzies did it.

Menzies and education reform

Menzies' contributions to education have been widely acknowledged, notwithstanding the caveats noted above. It is significant when asked on his retirement to list his lasting achievements[149] Menzies nominated "what has been done about education".[150]

There are four noteworthy issues about Menzies and education.

First, Menzies had a personal and genuine interest in education long prior to his second term as prime minister. His first broadcast to the nation as prime minister referenced earlier highlighted his own considerable education achievements and its importance to his career progression. His "Forgotten People" broadcasts are peppered with references to education issues. Following the war, he noted, "the most fundamental task in front of us is to educate a new generation".[151] His commitment to education also partly reflected his Scottish Presbyterian upbringing.

Second, as Leader of the Opposition Menzies in 1945 "initiated the first major debate on education in the federal parliament".[152] His keynote speech[153] outlined farsighted proposals for education including: increased facilities and funding across almost all parts of education from schools, adult education, universities, even pre-schools, and to address issues concerning qualifications, status and remuneration of teachers. Although education was constitutionally a state responsibility, Menzies predicted and thought it desirable, that "the Commonwealth will, in all probability, be a substantial contributor to educational reform".[154] He had no qualms about considering using Section 96 of the Constitution for Commonwealth funding to the states to overcome the Constitution's limitations. He called for "the Commonwealth to establish forthwith, in collaboration with the states, a highly competent committee or commission to investigate the problem and submit recommendations".[155] These ideas were to manifest themselves in concrete policy initiatives during his prime ministership.

Third, in office Menzies took action, initially on universities, but later on schools. He retained Labor's, Office of Education and its key personnel and it became part of the new expanded Department of Prime Minister and Cabinet. In 1950 he appointed in an inquiry into university funding partly begun by his predecessor and quickly implemented its recommendations for increased Commonwealth funding to the sector. The hiatus till the next major initiative six years later probably reflected the four elections Menzies faced (1949, 1951, 1954 and 1955). It was not until the last of these that Menzies felt secure and had the time to focus on major new policy initiatives. Hence, in 1956 he appointed the *Committee on Australian Universities* chaired by Sir Keith Murray. This was the real turning point in university education in Australia. It was the first full scale review of university education. This, and the subsequent 1961 *Committee on the Future of Tertiary Education in Australia*[56] chaired by Sir Leslie Martin resulted in: large increases in Commonwealth funding; the establishment of the binary system; formation of the statutory based Australian Universities Commission (1959); a research grants scheme; and a large expansion of Commonwealth student scholarships. Funding for universities increased by tenfold between 1955 and 1966. University enrolments rose from 16,500 in 1945 to 81,400 by 1965. There was a huge expansion of the Commonwealth Scholarship Scheme that had been made possible by Labor's successful 1946 Constitutional referendum that had given power to the Commonwealth to provide "benefits to students." By 1963 some 37 per cent of students had their university fees paid and had access to a means-tested living allowance. Following implementation of the Martin Report 75 per cent of all tertiary students had their education paid for by the Commonwealth. Menzies may not have been quite the originator of these initiatives as he later contended,[157] but once convinced of their value he became their major driver, involved in all aspects of the reviews and ensured their implementation. Menzies established Australia's modern tertiary education sector. As Labor leader Gough Whitlam was later to admit: "No Australian has done more to serve the cause of university education in this country than Sir Robert Menzies".[158]

Lastly, Menzies tackled in his final term (1963-66), the 'state-aid' issue – public funding of non-government schools – independent and Catholic. This issue had bedevilled both parties in different ways. For Labor the issue was an ideological one. It was opposed to supporting private schools including the largest and poorest part of that sector – Catholic schools. Labor's mantra was free, compulsory and secular public education – even though Labor drew the bulk of Australia's large Catholic population's vote and many of its members and leaders were of that faith.[159] For Liberals, funding any schools meant Commonwealth intrusion into what was constitutionally, a state responsibility – a dangerous precedent for federalists. Their added problem was that as an essentially

Protestant party, funding the non-government sector would inevitably mean supporting Catholic schools. At a time when sectarianism[160] was rife, this was abhorrent to many, including some Liberals.

The first step to ending the state-aid conundrum was funding non-government schools, including Catholic ones in the ACT when it was still run directly by the Commonwealth. Menzies' logic for this was impeccable and praiseworthy.[161] This raised few objections. There were also tax deductions for parents who sent children to private schools. However, it was at the 1963 election when Menzies announced, to the surprise of many in his own party, what was to become the beginning of Commonwealth funding to both non-government and state public schools. This involved a special competitive Commonwealth Scholarships to assist students to complete grades 11 and 12 – and significantly for all students "without discrimination".[162] In addition, grants for secondary school science facilities – again for all schools public and private. These science facilities grants were the first time the Commonwealth funded schools directly, as distinct, from supporting students. There was also increased support for technical colleges. This was the beginning of the end of the state-aid issue. Support for non-government schools was to become bipartisan policy as was ever increasing Commonwealth involvement in schools.

Menzies started it.

Menzies cleverly took one other initiative that

reflected his judgement of people and which assisted in the implementation of these ground-breaking changes. Following the successful 1963 election, Menzies in 1964 made Senator John Gorton Minister for Works. However, Gorton was given an additional role as "Minister assisting the Prime Minister in Commonwealth activities relating to research and education".[163] This, Menzies told Gorton, was his "real role" and this was clearly outlined in Gorton's letter of appointment.[164] Menzies understood how ambitious and motivated Gorton was ("He wants to be Prime Minister" he told Barwick in 1964)[165] and assessed he would tackle this important task diligently. Administratively, Gorton was responsible for the Commonwealth Office of Education in the Prime Minister's Department, the Australian National University, the National Library, the Australian Universities Commission and the CSIRO. More importantly, it involved implementing the changes about school funding and training. Gorton had to develop new legislation and negotiate with the states and with the non-government sector. Gorton was effective in implementing these changes. Menzies had appointed the right person to achieve his policy. After Menzies retired Gorton was elevated to cabinet under Prime Minster Holt and became Australia's first federal Minister for Education and Science. In December 1966 the Commonwealth Department of Education and Science was at last established as a formal department of state. It remains one of the Commonwealth's key departments. Menzies may have retired by then, but there should be no doubt that its formation was a testimony to his efforts.

Menzies foray into schools was motivated by the best of intentions and clear principles – of giving choice to parents, and that every child, regardless of background, should receive government support for education. However, it was not without its political goals. The Coalition was seeking a greater share the Catholic vote (and Democratic Labor Party preferences). The policy also caused disarray within the Labor Party. It had to grapple with wanting to maintain its ideological purity of resisting funding to non-government schools, while trying to respond to a popular policy introduced by its opponent that was taking votes from its base. While these initial changes in school funding did not bring the immediate bonanza in funding that some in the non-government sector expected,[166] it was an important beginning of increased Commonwealth funding that proved to be unstoppable. Perhaps, if Menzies had known that by 2020 the Commonwealth would be the largest single funder of schools in Australia, based on a complex formula that few understand, he may have been less enthusiastic. He may have preferred to have limited Commonwealth education involvement to the tertiary sector. Nevertheless, it was Menzies and the Liberals which took the key education initiatives during this period. It is Menzies who most deserves the title of the 'Education Prime Minister.' Former Labor Treasurer and leader, Bill Hayden, best sums up the Menzies' education legacy especially in relation to the state-aid issue:

> Though a Presbyterian in good standing with his Church, Menzies ... did the very thing his Church counselled against. In public funding science blocks and libraries for non-State schools, Church and State were hand in glove in a way they had not been for ninety years. Menzies' tactic was to propitiate the DLP and hold their preference votes, garner Catholic support for his party and divide Labor ... Whitlam fought doggedly to establish broad community support for State Aid and he was certainly successful, but it was a Presbyterian, Menzies who was the initial architect.[167]

Menzies and international affairs[168]

The Menzies Government's foreign affairs policies needs to be understood in the context of the 'Cold War' that developed after the end of World War Two which quickly saw Europe divided by what Churchill called the "iron curtain" and real conflict between the great powers of the United States and the USSR. Often this manifested itself in 'small wars' – insurgencies, guerrilla wars, and wars of national liberation. These challenges were not confined to areas of decolonialisation in Africa. There were real threats in nearby Asia. All this required a deft hand and what Kissinger called, "realpolitik – foreign policy based on calculations of power and national interest".[169] Menzies provided skilful guidance through these difficult and complex times that is little appreciated.

Although Menzies remained a strong supporter of the Commonwealth of Nations – never missing its meetings, and personally liking things British, he was forever the political realist when it came to international relations and developing trends. Australia's national interests were always put first. While he played the circuses with the British Commonwealth and organising visits of the young and popular Queen Elizabeth II to Australia, his ministers and policy directions were elsewhere.

Menzies reaffirmed the alliance with the United States begun by Labor Prime Minister Curtin during World War Two as the signing of the ANZUS Treaty in 1951 testified. On his retirement Menzies listed this as the "best single step that had been taken in the time of my government".[170] This reorientation to the United States was further seen during the 1960s when Australia even stopped buying British planes for its defence and purchased instead the controversial F-111 from General Dynamics of the United States along with other procurement decisions.

At the same time Australia during this time became increasingly involved in Asian issues, sometimes under the auspices of the United Nations as seen in the Korean War (1950), or in support of the United Kingdom with the Malayan Emergency (1948-60) that broke the back of a pro-Beijing insurgency and allowed peninsula Malaya to become independent in 1957. Later it would support the United States in the Vietnam War (1965). However, the Colombo Plan was Australia's own initiative and so too was the support Australia gave to the fledging Malaysian state during the Indonesian Confrontation (1963-66).

This reorientation away from the United Kingdom to Asia was also seen in trade. In 1950 a third of Australia's exports were sold to the UK. By 1964 this had been halved (15 per cent). Japan became Australia's biggest single trading partner along with other developing countries of the region. The 1957 *Australia-Japan Agreement on Commerce* largely developed by McEwen reflected this new direction. Despite foreign policy constraints and ideological concerns in recognising the People's Republic of China (PRC), the pragmatic Menzies, urged on by the even more pragmatic Country Party, ensured that Australia sold wheat and wool to that vast market. However, Menzies was never keen for total rapprochement with the PRC. That issue only became more pressing after his retirement.

Unlike New Zealand, Australia early on sensed Britain's loss of interest and power 'East of Suez' and her inevitable drift to Europe especially after the formation of the European Economic Community (EEC) in 1957 which Britain sought to join in 1961. So, under the ever energetic McEwen, Australia began to seek alternative markets.

Menzies was highly regarded by overseas leaders. His

meetings with Truman, Eisenhower, Kennedy, Johnson and Nixon and the respect in which he was held, went beyond diplomatic courtesies. In the United Kingdom honours were bestowed on him, but the real reflection of British esteem was when he spoke at Sir Winston Churchill's memorial service at St Paul's Cathedral. Yet, "this important moment in Australia's modern history is all but lost, collateral damage of our politics"[171].

While Menzies may not have had quite the same rapport with some of the leaders of emerging Asian countries, he visited the region often, and Australia was involved in their economic development and as highlighted, their protection against Communism. For Lee Kuan Yew, leader of Singapore from 1959 to 1990, the Australian prime minister who impressed him the most was Menzies and the least, Whitlam. As Lee Kuan Yew wrote about Menzies following his death:

> He was an outstanding leader ... he presided over two decades of growth ... His great stature was justly deserved. A man fiercely proud of Australia's links with Britain, he was also a realist who set out painstakingly to build up Australia's links with the new countries in Asia, particularly immediate neighbours in South-East Asia.[172]

Robert Murray summed up the Menzies' achievement in foreign affairs especially in relation to the region:

> Contrary to modern myth making, Australia's role in the Menzies era from 1949 to 1966 was very much in Asia and the Pacific region, not the fading empire

> (British). That was the period when the foundations of the modern Asia-Pacific region were laid and Menzies' governments pioneered most of the Australian moves into it.[173]

Let's leave it at that.

Menzies and modernising Australian government

It was during this period under Menzies that in response to numerous challenges and change that "the foundations of Australia as it will enter the 21st century were firmly laid"[174] This involved Australia securing its place in the world and the maturing of its national system of government and the operations of the federal system. After all, Australia as a federated nation was just a half century old when Menzies came to power in 1949. The structure and pattern of Australian government was to be resolved and set during this period. It was part of Menzies' legacy that the Commonwealth Government (now the Australian Government), confirmed its national primacy in both government and politics.

Menzies although a federalist, had since the 1940s eschewed the notion that Australia's national direction or unity would be sacrificed on the altar of states' rights and parochial political concerns. He essentially accepted the trend that had gained momentum under Labor and was necessitated by modern economic management, of increased Commonwealth taxation powers, and involvement in areas that were constitutionally state responsibilities. Under Menzies, the pattern of federal-state relations involving growing Commonwealth fiscal dominance, and increasing use of Section 96 specific purpose grants, was set. The overriding supremacy of the national government's wishes was firmly and unassailably established. It did not all start with Whitlam. This, as we have noted, was seen in areas such as education and housing, but also increasingly included other areas like health, transport, aviation, agriculture and communications to name but a few. Although the Premiers' Conference with the Commonwealth at its head had been operating since the 1920s, it was during this period that federal-state ministerial councils on different areas of policy began to grow in number and importance with increasing Commonwealth leadership.[175] The invitation in 1965 by the state education ministers for their Commonwealth counterpart, Senator Gorton, to join the Australian Education Council, set the pattern in the future for other policy areas.

Concerning the public service[176] when Menzies came to office in 1949 he inherited as a legacy of the war years and post war reconstruction, a greatly expanded public service. National government had also become involved in more areas than when he was last prime minister. There were legitimate concerns about the growth of the public service given its rapid expansion and creation of many new departments and agencies as well as its coherence. For a new incoming government there were understandable concerns about the loyalty of senior public servants who had served nearly eight years under Labor administrations. At the same time there was the need to recruit into the public service people of quality and to attract them to Canberra.

Menzies was a strict adherent to the Westminster system of government with its professional, independent, and neutral public service providing 'frank and fearless' advice. In office, he practised what he preached. He kept most of the senior public servants inherited from Labor. This was seen in how Dr H.C. Coombs, appointed by Labor as Secretary of the Department of Post War Reconstruction and then head of the Commonwealth Bank, was retained, became a trusted adviser and as mentioned above, became Governor of the Reserve Bank in 1960. As Thompson said, because of this approach, "the senior ranks of the Commonwealth Public Service under Menzies were filled with men of outstanding ability who commanded the respect of leaders in the business and professional world".[177] The public service's independence was buttressed by its permanent career structure and a strong independent Public Service Board.

Menzies did pursue economies. He cut 10,000 from Commonwealth employment in 1951 given that numbers had risen from 100,000 in 1946 to 158,000 by 1950 – a 58 per cent increase. Thereafter, the public service grew steadily, but at a far slower rate than previously – just 3 per cent per annum so that by 1960 numbers stood at 163,000. Public Service employment stabilised at about 5 per cent of civilian and defence employment throughout the Menzies era. Nevertheless, the number of government departments gradually increased during this period.

Menzies was never into fads. There was some privatisation of government enterprises in his first term, but it never became an obsession. As discussed in relation to the two- airline policy, where it was practical and necessary to retain a government enterprise it was kept. Overall, by the 1980s when privatisation became a major issue Australia at the national level had far fewer of these bodies compared to some other countries, and less than across the states.

Nor was Menzies enamoured with that other consumer item of modern government – the public inquiry in either royal commission or non-statutory form. He resisted holding a major public inquiry (a royal commission was called)[178] into the public service as occurred overseas (USA, Canada, New Zealand and Eire).[179] Menzies used public inquiries sparingly and judiciously. Over sixteen years only five royal commissions and thirty public inquiries were appointed. It was not in Menzies' style to, as he said, "to offload the responsibility on to two or three people who are outside of government" to decide "what functions the government could perform"[180]. The two aforementioned public inquiries into tertiary education were about genuinely seeking expert advice to inform government on an important new area of public policy. Subsequent governments. starting with Whitlam and followed by Coalition governments, greatly expanded the use of these mechanisms – sometimes with adverse consequences.[181]

However, to improve public service recruitment the Menzies Government appointed in 1956 the Boyer Committee into Public Service Recruitment (the timing is again significant). Although many of its recommendations were initially rejected concerning establishing a new administrative class, ending the marriage bar, and making graduate recruitment easier, progress did occur so that by the end of Menzies' term most of Boyer's proposals had been implemented.[182]

Overall, Menzies was not enthusiastic about large-scale restructurings of the public bureaucracy or excessive tinkering with administrative arrangements. On coming to office he abolished Labor's Post War Reconstruction Department which Chifley had started to do. He later split the Department of Supply and transferred munitions production to a new Department of Defence Production. The 1949 election promise for a new Department of National Development was kept, but its role was to be circumscribed by other departments under Country Party ministers. Menzies implemented proposals for a Cabinet Secretariat within the Department of Prime Minister. Cabinet processes were routinised, and in 1955 Cabinet was split to into inner and outer ministries, a practice followed today.

Menzies' ministry also exuded stability. Frequent ministerial reshuffles were avoided. During Menzies second prime-ministership there were only two Treasurers – Fadden and Holt. McEwen was initially Minister for Commerce and Agriculture and then Trade Minister from 1958 until he retired in 1971. Hasluck was Minister for Territories for twelve years. Casey was at External Affairs for nearly nine. Even when Menzies knew that a minister like William McMahon may have leaked cabinet information, he took action to warn,[183] he rarely sacked.[184] He also retained a number of small departments which could be used to train and assess junior minsters.

Menzies' other achievement in modernising government was his decisions concerning Canberra, the nation's capital. Until he came to office Canberra's development had been sporadic. It was Menzies' decision to move the remainder of the federal bureaucracy, much of which was still lingering in Melbourne and Sydney, to Canberra. By so doing, Menzies made Canberra a true modern capital of the nation, assisted by his support of the National Capital Development Corporation with appropriate resourcing and a competent leader in the form of John Overall, as its first commissioner (1957-72). As Canberra journalist Wallace Brown highlighted, it was Menzies who:

> ... shifted thousands of stubborn public servants from Melbourne and Sydney. Proceeded with Walter Griffith's plan to form an artificial lake ... and

> turned a bush town of 10 suburbs into a lovely city of which all Australians can be proud. All this was achieved in the face of significant opposition and criticism from business and electors.[185]

Menzies was always proud of this achievement for Canberra even if it was not always appreciated when he went out into some of the distant regions where funding and resources were less bountiful.[186]

If stability was a hallmark of the Menzies' second prime ministership then it could not have occurred if relations with the Country Party had not been placed on a more secure and cordial basis than during his first prime ministership. Menzies, as noted, had learnt a lot from that time. There were challenges. Menzies had to deal with some formidable Country Party leaders, especially McEwen. This was partly on policy matters. The Liberals had concerns at McEwen's expanding tariff protection policies, while he in turn was worried about the Liberals' approach to foreign investment. The clash over the Vernon Report has been noted. The Country Party lost Treasury after Fadden's retirement in 1958. Menzies resisted McEwen's pressure after the 1961 election to expand his portfolio of Trade and Industry. There was also electoral competition between the two parties with numerous three corner contests, disputes over electoral redistributions (which largely favoured the Country Party), joint senate tickets and election promises. As many of these electoral matters were decided at the state party organisational levels the national parliamentary leaders could not always impose their wills. What has been called Menzies' 'indulgence' to the Country Party on both policy and electoral issues was largely correct, with exceptions noted, but it paid off. As Professor Brian Costar summed up:

> Had Menzies been less astute and publicly confronted McEwen on each and every occasion which warranted it, it is doubtful that the coalition would have survived intact for as long as it did.[187]

After Menzies retired relations between the parties would become more tense as subsequent Liberal prime ministers lost their electoral appeal and stature and policy differences became more distinct. This was partly driven by bureaucratic rivalries, and as always in politics, nourished by personal dislike as between Liberal Treasurer McMahon and Trade Minister, McEwen.

There was something else about the Menzies era worth noting. Scandals were unknown. Nethercote reminds us that during these years "there was only one case of a ministerial resignation stemming from … a conflict of interest"[188] – that concerned John Lawson, Minister for Trade and Customs had to resign after winning stakes with a race horse rented from a leading industrialist who had gained a lucrative motorcar manufacturing monopoly from the Government. Wallace Brown sums up both Menzies' and his government's integrity:

> Menzies' … hallmark was his great contribution to clean government. His personal integrity was unquestioned and there were no signs of corruption

in his administration. He oversaw and set standards for an impartial public service.[189]

When Menzies retired to Melbourne he was not a person of wealth. Consequently, a group of well-wishers donated funds for Menzies and his wife to purchase a house. The Menzies accepted on condition that once they became too old to live there or died, it was to be sold and the proceeds were to go to two schools. In other words, the gift was not to accrue wealth to the Menzies family in any way. And that is exactly what happened. Indeed, journalist Kenneth Davidson of *The Age* after Paul Keating had made denigrating comments about Menzies in 1994 noted that:

> Sir Robert Menzies retired no richer than when he entered public life. Mr Hawke and Mr Keating are the only Australian prime ministers to become very rich men after entering public life.[190]

Conclusions

Australia under Menzies was not as dull as is now depicted by too many with little regard to the context of the times or comparisons with other like countries. While it was a different era from now, it was a period when a young nation was effused with a sense of vitality. It was marked by changes in politics, public policy and social life. Many of the transitions that began during this period were nurtured and went on to lay the foundations for a more modern, and in many ways, different Australia, later. Certainly, new concerns, interests, issues and groups have emerged since those times. Nevertheless, this does not diminish the contributions that Menzies and his governments made to allow these transitions to occur with the minimum of disruption.

Indeed, Menzies' real achievement was giving a sense of stability and reassurance at this time of great change. This was achieved by his "personal demeanour" which "conveyed such an air of stability and reassurance" which, combined with his open display to Australia's traditional links, such as Britain and the Commonwealth, "gave the community a sense of continuity with the past and to the new arrivals that they were part of a society that had some heritage and tradition of its own".[191] It allowed the many changes affecting Australia at the time to be absorbed with little alarm. This has not been understood by Menzies' critics.

Not all on the Labor side were as poisonous as Keating repeatedly was, or as dismissive as Horne. Gough Whitlam on Menzies' 80th birthday graciously acknowledged his core qualities:

> In his recent writings, Sir Robert has expressed his deep respect and affection for the Australian people – 'an intelligent, good and decent people.' For a people not noted for the awe in which they hold their political leaders, they have returned that respect and affection in rare measure.[192]

Professor Colin Hughes too, thought that a more

"balanced ... indeed quite possibly the best assessment"[193] of Menzies, in contrast to Horne's "savage" critique, was by Dr Jim Cairns, long time left of centre federal Labor politician and at one time Deputy Prime Minister in the Whitlam Government. After a personal meeting with Menzies towards the end of his term in office Cairns said:

> Sir Robert Menzies was one of the most effective politicians in Australia's history. He had a way of identifying the attitudes of average Australians and appealing very vividly, clearly, and incisively to those attitudes, showing a skill and understanding that I didn't expect he had.
>
> He didn't appear to have the common touch. I thought he was consciously or naturally aristocratic and it surprised me to find he had an ability to know what the average man felt. I don't know how he did this, but I would say he had a good deal of natural flair for it.
>
> The second thing that surprised me is that I thought he liked to exercise power, but I am now pretty sure that he did not, that he tried to avoid it and put things off ... He was, I feel, exercising the role of an actor. I think Menzies was a man who liked the spotlight, who appreciated an audience. I would think that being a thespian in many ways gave him much of his satisfaction.[194]

The late Clive James, Australia's much praised international journalist, broadcaster and writer when reviewing John Howard's recent portrayal of Menzies[195] put Menzies' critics in perspective:

> Generations of Australia's inner city intellectuals were later to indulge in the fond belief that Menzies had no mind at all, just a set of patrician instincts by which he stole from the poor and bowed in the directions of the Queen. Some of them still think that … Nowadays anyone with an IQ above a skin temperature realize that Menzies, if only for the results that he obtained, must have had something complex going on behind that magnificent set of eyebrows.[196]

What has really gnawed at Menzies' detractors was not his policies, or the alleged lack of them, or his so called 'Britishness', or his perceived patrician style, or even his supposed lack of vision. No, what really hurt, what really drove them to distraction, what made it so essential that he had to be denigrated, side-lined, besmirched and now ignored, was that he beat them. He won. Over and over he had the toughness and resilience to come back from near political death. He overcame the ignominy of his first failed prime-ministership and after retreating to the backbench to "bleed a while" went on to establish a new political party out of a fractious rabble – a political party that still endures, and nationally is Australia's most successful. He kept on after the Liberal Party's failed first outing at the 1946 federal election. In 1951 he held Australia's only second double dissolution and not only won, but also gained control of the Senate that Labor had changed the rules to thwart his expected win in 1949. Later in 1951 he bounced back from defeat of the referendum. He was able to exploit the opportunities presented by the Petrov affair and expose Evatt's political ineptness, delusion and lack of leadership. Again, after his near loss at the 1961 election, he showed hardly any loss of face, re-asserted his leadership, learnt from the mistakes, refocused and developed new policies – including some borrowed from the opposition. He instigated the beginning of funding to non-government schools and thus started the end of the 'state-aid' controversy that had dogged education policy for decades and then took these to the 1963 election which he won comfortably.

In politics, despite all the emphasis about principles, platforms and visions, it is winning that ultimately counts for all sides. Parties exist to win, to gain power. All politicians yearn for office. Those who say they don't are deluding themselves, their supporters and the public. And that is what his detractors cannot stand most about Menzies – he beat them. He kept them out. In particular, he denied Labor its supposed momentum of history. He was stable and pragmatic, he moved with the times. His Labor rivals remained chained to outdated dogma like nationalisation of industry, more public ownership, public housing, and a concept of class war rather than individual freedom, choice and initiative. Labor stuck with leaders whom they knew had become mentally unfit for any office.

Worst of all, by Menzies choosing his own time of retirement he robbed his detractors of the satisfaction of seeing him defeated. As Clive James said, by this alone Menzies "probably animated his detractors far more than almost any single piece of policy linked with the Menzies era".[197]

But let us close this brief overview of a great political leader with how he himself announced his retirement from office and quietly exited from public view. It says a lot about Menzies' own astute awareness of his age, his limitations, and the changing nature of Australian politics which was slipping away from his own life experiences. It also highlights an honesty about himself which he was willing to share with the Australian people that few of his successors ever achieved except in tearful defeat:

> I have given thought to my future in the light of what seems best for the Government and the country. In the result I have decided to resign from the Prime Ministership forthwith.
>
> Since I became leader of the Opposition at the end of 1943 I have been responsible for the conduct of no less than eight general elections in addition to two separate Senate elections. The strain of election campaigns is something that the onlooker cannot be expected fully to understand.
>
> Meanwhile, the complexities of government, both domestic and international, have grown enormously.

It would be idle for me to pretend that all these years and tasks have not affected me …

In short, I am tired: my pace has slowed down; I could not properly continue in office for very much longer and at the same time do justice to the growing problems of the nation.

By the normal date of the next election, in December of this year, I would be 72 years old. Feeling as I do, I would not be justified in asking the people to re-elect me for a further term. It would not be fair to them, or, for that matter to myself. For I would not be willing to contest such an election without having decided that, if successful, I would remain for about two years at least after the election. To do otherwise would be unthinkable and electorally deceptive.

I hope that the people, not only in the government parties but all over Australia, will accept my announcement as one of a decision taken after deep and anxious thought, weighing my duties properly, and with the interests of our country, in a period of rapid change and acute problems, much in my heart and mind. Beyond doubt, the affairs of the world at large, and of Australia in a period of dramatic development, are increasing in weight and complexity. They demand the services of men and women of full vigour and flexibility of mind, feeling at their best and able to do their best.[198]

Indeed, as stated at the beginning of this monograph, there will never be another Menzies.

Notes

1   Andrew Barton, Australia's first prime minister retired from politics in 1903 to join the High Court. Labor prime minister Andrew Fisher retired of his own accord in 1915 and went on to become High Commissioner to the United Kingdom.

2   Paul 't Hart, "How Adenauer Lost Power: Understanding Leadership Rivalry and Succession Conflict in Political Parties," *German Politics*, Vol 16, No 2, June, 2007, pp. 273-291.

3   Francis Clarke, *Australia: A Concise Political and Social History*, Oxford University Press, Melbourne, 1989, pp. 233-234.

4   Donald Horne, *The Lucky Country*, Penguin, Ringwood, 1965, pp. 187-9.

5   Donald Horne, "Endurance – but what did it mean?" *The Australian*, 20-21 May 1978.

6   Paul Keating MP, "How Menzies failed Australia," *Sydney Morning Herald*, 28 October 1994.

7   Keating, "How Menzies failed Australia," 1994.

8   Paul Keating MP, "The Challenge of Public Policy," Address, 15 May 1991.

9   Paul Keating MP, Launch of John Curtin's War, Lowy Institute, 27 November 2017; for a response see Gerald Henderson, "Keating's 'woeful coward' slur against Menzies ignores historical truths," *The Australian*, 2 December 2017.

10 Henry Ergas and Jonathan Pincus, "The Wealth of the Nation," in John Nethercote, (ed), *Menzies: The Shaping of Modern Australia*, Connor Court Publishing, Redland Bay, p. 164.

11 Judith Brett, "Menzies R.G.," in Brian Galligan and Winsome Roberts, (eds), *The Oxford Companion to Australian Politics*, Oxford University Press, Melbourne, 2007, p. 339.

12 Troy Bramston, *Robert Menzies – The Art of Politics*, Scribe Publications, Brunswick, 2019, p, 311.

13 Gwen Gray, "Social Policy," in Scott Prasser, John Nethercote and John Warhurst, (eds), *The Menzies Era: A Reappraisal of Government, Politics, and Policy*, Hale & Iremonger, Sydney, 1995, p. 211.

14 Gray, "Social Policy," p. 223.

15 Keating, "How Menzies failed Australia," 1994.

16 Simon Marginson, "The Whitlam Government and Education," in Jenny Hocking and Colleen Lewis, (eds), *Whitlam and Modern Labor: It's Time Again*, Melbourne Publishing Group, Melbourne, 2003, pp. 244-272.

17 Gough Whitlam MP, *Commonwealth Parliamentary Debates*, House of Representatives, 'Tertiary education in Australia,' 29 April, 1965.

18 Janice Reid (Vice Chancellor UWS), "Menzies, Whitlam, and Social Justice: A View from the Academy," *The 2012 Sir Robert Menzies Oration on Higher Education*, University of Melbourne, Melbourne, p. 6.

19 Gough Whitlam, *The Whitlam Government 1972-1975*, Penguin Books, Ringwood, 1985, pp. 292-311.

20 Ian Wilkinson, Brian Caldwell, RJW Selleck, Jessica Harris, Pam Denman, *A History of State Aid to Non-Government Schools in Australia*, Department of Education, Science and Training, Canberra, September 2006.

21 Tony Taylor, *Class Wars: Money, Schools and Power in Modern Australia*, Monash University, Melbourne, 2018, pp. 31-44.

22 Russel Ward, *Australia: A Short History*, Ure Smith, Sydney, 1969, p. 166.

23 Graeme Starr, "The Old Man on the Stairs: The Menzies of Myth and Legend," in Prasser et al, *The Menzies Era*, p. 53.

24 Graham Maddox, "The Australian Labor Party," in Graeme Starr, Keith Richmond, and Graham Maddox, (eds), *Political Parties in Australia*, Heinemann Educational Australia, Sydney, 1978, p. 160.

25 Henry Mayer, "Some conceptions of the Australian party system 1910-1950," *Historical Studies, Australia and New Zealand*, Vol 7, November 1956, pp. 253-70 and several times subsequently.

26 Humphrey McQueen,"Menzies," in *Gallipoli to Petrov*, Allen and Unwin, Sydney, pp. 174-5.

27 McQueen, *Gallipoli to Petrov*, p.175.

28 Horne, "Endurance," 1978.

29 John Carroll, "The Battle for Sir Robert Menzies: Rewriting our History," *Quadrant*, XIX, 1-2, January-February 1985, p. 66.

30 Paddy McGuinness, "Menzies: Great or Not?' *Sydney Morning Herald*, 8 October 1994.

31 Sir John Bunting, *R.G. Menzies: A Portrait*, Allen & Unwin, Sydney, 1988.

32 Don Whitington, *The Rulers: Fifteen Years of the Liberals*, Landsdowne Press, Melbourne, Revised edition, 1965.

33 Michelle Grattan, "An old retainer pays tribute to the memory of his master," *The Australian*, 19 May 1988.

34 Jefferson Penberthy, "When will we learn the truth about Menzies?' *Sydney Morning Herald*, 5 September 1981.

35 Bramston, *Robert Menzies*, pp. 1-4.

36 Menzies, *Afternoon Light: Some Memories of Men and Events*, Cassell, London 1967, p 1.

37 Ross Fitzgerald, "Erudite portrait," *Courier-Mail*, 20 November 1999.

38 Allan Martin, *Robert Menzies: A Life, Volume 1 –1894-1943*, Melbourne University Press, Melbourne, 1993; *Robert Menzies: A Life, Volume 2 –1944-1978*, Melbourne University Press, Melbourne 1999.

39 Graeme Starr, "The Old Man on the Stairs," pp. 44-54.

40 Gerard Henderson, *Menzies' Child: The Liberal Party of Australia 1944-1994*, Allen & Unwin, Sydney, 1994, p. 71.

41 Elena Douglas, "Rethinking History; The Stolen Legacy," *Australian Financial Review*, 24 January 2014.

42 Douglas, "Rethinking History," 2014.

43 Norman Abjorensen, "Australia's top 10 PMs," *Canberra Times*, 5 December 1992.

44 Tony Walker and Albert J. Joutsoukis, "The good, the bad, and the couldabeens," *Australian Financial Review*, 3 January 2001.

45 Michael Gordon and Michelle Grattan, "Curtin our greatest PM," *The Age*, 18 December 2004.

46 Paul Strangio, "Evaluating Prime-Ministerial Performance: The Australian Experience," in Paul Srangio, Paul 't Hart and James Walter, (eds), *Understanding Prime-Ministerial Performance: Comparative Perspectives*, Oxford University Press, Oxford, 2013, pp, 279-80.

47 Patrick Weller, *The Prime Ministers' Craft: Why Some Succeed and Others Fail in Westminster Systems*, Oxford University Press, Oxford, 2018, p. 22.

48 Ibid.

49 Ibid.

50 Ibid.

51 Ibid.

52 This section acknowledges Allan Martin and Patsy Hardy, (eds), *Dark and Hurrying Days: Menzies 1941 Diary*, National Library of Australia, Canberra, 1993.

53 *The Age*, 27 April 1939.

54 Allan Martin, *Robert Menzies Volume 1*, p. 138-9.

55 Don Rawson, *Australia Votes: The 1958 Federal Election*, Melbourne University Press, Melbourne, 1961.

56 Allan Martin, "Sir Robert Gordon Menzies," in Michelle Grattan, (ed), *Australian Prime Ministers*, New Holland Australia, Melbourne, 2000, p. 204.

57 Evatt was a brilliant lawyer, born in 1894 in NSW (same year as Menzies), served in state politics, elevated to the High Court in 1930, entered federal parliament in 1940 and became leader of the federal Labor Party in 1951 – a position he held till he retired and appointed to the NSW Supreme Court in 1960. He died in 1965.

58 Australian Dictionary of Biography, "Dame Pattie Maie Menzies," 1895-1995.

59 Robert Menzies, "Politics, 'Fine Art and Inexact Science'" *The New York Times Magazine*, 28 November 1948.

60 Labor's Treasurer, former Queensland Labor Premier E.G. Theodore had to stand down pending a Queensland royal commission into his and another former Labor premier's alleged corruption concerning the purchase of the Mungana mine. Although found that they had acted in collusion to profit dishonestly at the Crown's expense, subsequent legal action failed and Theodore returned as Treasurer. This was one of the factors that provoked Lyons to leave the Labor Party. See Kett Kennedy, *The Mungana Affair*, University of Queensland, St Lucia, 1978.

61 Don Whitington, *The House Will Divide: A Review of Australian Federal Politics*, Georgian House, Melbourne, 1954, p. 53.

62 Dame Enid Lyons, *Among the Carrion Crows Rigby, Adelaide, 1972* quoted in Paul Kelly, "Menzies: The Man and the Myth," *National Times*, 27 May 1978, p. 9.

63 Quoted in Kevin Perkins, *Menzies: The Last of the Queen's Men*, Angus & Robertson, London, 1968, p. 75.

64 Menzies, *Afternoon Light*, p. 56.

65 Menzies, *Afternoon Light*, p. 15.

66 Martin and Hardy, *Dark and Hurrying Days*, 1993.

67 Menzies, *Afternoon Light*, p. 56.

68 Quoted in Anne Henderson, *Menzies at War*, UNSW Press, Sydney, 2014, p. 56.

69 Stephen Roberts, *The House that Hitler Built*, Harper and Brothers, London, 1938.

70 See Gerard Henderson,"Keating's 'woeful slur' against Menzies ignores historical truths," *The Australian*, 2 December 2017, for discussion concerning Keating's attacks.

71 See Henderson, *Menzies at War*, 2014; Martin, *Robert Menzies: A Life, Volume 1*, pp. 337-355.

72 Paul Hasluck, *The Government and the People, 1939-1941* quoted in Paul Kelly, "Menzies – The Man and The Myth," *National Times*, 27 May 1978.

73 Menzies, *Afternoon Light*, p. 57.

74 Menzies, *Afternoon Light*, p. 57.

75 Paul Kelly, "How the politician learned from his mistakes," *National Times*, 27 May 1978.

76 Menzies, *Afternoon Light*, p. 286.

77 Gerard Henderson, *Menzies' Child*, pp. 61-89.

78 Quoted in Ian Hancock, *The Liberals: The NSW Division 1945-2000*, Federation Press, Sydney, 2007, p. 64.

79 Robert Menzies, *The Forgotten People and Other Studies in Democracy*, Angus & Robertson, Sydney, 1943.

80 See Clem Lloyd, "The Media," in Prasser et al, *The Menzies Era*, pp.111-122 and p.119.

81 Robert Menzies, *Central Power in the Australian Commonwealth: An Examination of the Growth of Commonwealth Power in the Australian Federation*, Cassell, London,1967; Robert Menzies, *The Measure of the Years*, Cassell, London, 1970.

82 Menzies, *Afternoon Light*, and *Measure of the Years*.

83 Robert Menzies, "Looking around at 80," *The Herald*, 14 December 1974.

84 Menzies, "Politics, 'Fine Art and Inexact Science'" *New York Times Magazine*, 1948.

85   Menzies, *The Measure of the Years*, p. 8.

86 Troy Bramston, "Art of Politics has gone missing," *The Australian*, 30 July 2012; Bramston, *Robert Menzies*, pp.169-188.

87 Robert Menzies, *First Statement of Political Faith and Aims*, 14 October 1944 see Graeme Starr *The Liberal Party of Australia: A Documentary History*, Drummond/Heinemann, Richmond, 1980, p. 90.

88 Menzies, *First Statement of Political Faith and Aims*, in Starr, *The Liberal Party of Australia*, p 91.

89 Ibid.

90 Menzies, "Address to the Liberal Party Federal Council," in Starr, *The Liberal Party of Australia*, p. 217.

91 Ibid.

92 Richard French, "Political Capital," *Representation*, Vol 47, No 2, 2011, pp. 215-230.

93 Scott Prasser and John Warhurst, "Uncertainty masked by prosperity," *The Week-End Australian*, 8-9 October 1994.

94 After 1949 immigrants came from an increasingly more diverse range of countries with some 60 per cent from continental Europe – Eastern Europe, Germany, Italy, Greece, Holland, and Yugoslavia.

95 Harold Macmillan PM, Address to Conservative Party Conference, 3 February 1960 – see Alistair Horne, *Harold Macmillan, 1957-1986, Volume II: Official biography*, Viking Press, New York: 1988, pp. 195-7.

96 Malcolm Mackerras, "Elections and Party Performance," in Prasser et al, *The Menzies Era*, pp. 65-68.

97 Ibid., pp. 60-79.

98 For further discussion of this see Mackerras, "Elections and Party performance," pp. 65-68.

99 Nicholas Whitlam and John Stubbs, *The Nest of Traitors: The Petrov Affair*, University of Queensland Press, St Lucia, 1985, best sums up the conspiracy view of the issue.

100 Robert Manne, *The Petrov Affair: Politics and Espionage,* Pergamon, Sydney, 1987; Allan Martin, "New Light on the Petrov Affair," *Quadrant*, June 1995, pp. 46-50; John Nethercote, "The Timing of the 1954 Election," *Quadrant*, June 1995, pp. 50-42; Paul Strangio, Paul 't Hart and James Walter, *The Pivot of Power: Australian Prime Ministers and Political Leadership 1949-2016*, Miegunyah Press, Melbourne, 2017, pp. 26-29.

101 William Hudson, "1951-72," in Frank Crowley, (ed), *A New History of Australia*, Heinemann, Melbourne, 1974, p. 510.

102 Evatt announced in parliament that he had telegrammed Molotov, the USSR Foreign Minister to ascertain if the Petrov documents were authentic and in effect if there were any Soviet spies in Australia – see Manne, *The Petrov Affair*, p. 259-260. .

103 Its correct title is the Royal Commission on Espionage.

104 Martin, *Robert Menzies Volume 2*, p. 153.

105 Solomon Davis, "Light on Menzies," *Journal of Commonwealth Studies*, Vol VIII, No 3, 1968, p. 237.

106 Mackerras, "Elections and Party performance," p. 64.

107 Henry Ergas and John J. Pincus, "The Wealth of the Nation," in Nethercote, *Menzies*, p 164.

108 The Snowy Mountains project was a hydro-electric power and irrigation scheme that began in October 1949. It employed at one stage 5,000 workers. Its value, as well as its environmental impacts, have been questioned in recent years (see David Clark, "The Snowy dream and reality," *The Australian*, 20 May 1983).

109 Full immigration started in 1949, but as noted above work on the Snowy Mountain Scheme only began in October 1949.

110 Evatt promised increases in most pensions, abolition of the means test, and increases in wages that would have result in a large increase in Commonwealth expenditure (See Hudson, "1951-72," p. 510).

111 Bramston, *Robert Menzies*, p. 234.

112 Arthur Calwell was deputy leader of the federal Labor parliamentary party from 1951-1960 and leader from 1960-67. He was a staunch supporter of the White Australia policy.

113 John Hirst, *Australian History in 7 Questions*, Black Inc, Collingwood, 2014, p. 157.

114 Selwyn Cornish, *The Evolution of Central Banking in Australia*, Reserve Bank, Sydney, 2010, p. 17.

115 Peter Forsyth, "Microeconomic Policy and the Two Airline Policy," in Prasser, et al, *The Menzies Era,* pp. 209.

116 Robert Menzies, *Commonwealth Parliamentary Debates*, (CPD), House of Representatives (HR), 21 September 1965, p. 1085.

117 Alan Wood, "Why Menzies should be congratulated," *The Australian*, 2 January 1996; see Greg Whitwell, "Economic Policy," in Prasser et al, *The Menzies Era*, pp. 176-77.

118 Geoffrey Bolton, *The Middle Way: 1942-1988*, Oxford History of Australia Vol 5, Oxford University Press, Oxford, 1993, p. 85.

119 Ergas and Pincus, "The Wealth of the Nation," p. 134.

120 Ibid.

121 Bruce McFarlane, *Economic Policy in Australia: The Case for Reform*, Cheshire, Melbourne, 1968 – described Australia's policy making as

"hydra-headed" planning with too many siloed decision making centres – eg Tariff Board, Trade and Industry Department, Treasury, Primary Industries Department and Conciliation and Arbitration Commission.

122 Ergas and Pincus, "The Wealth of the Nation," p. 134.

123 Hudson, "1951-72," p. 534.

124 Heinz Arndt, *A Small Rich Industrial Country: Studies in Australian Development, Aid and Trade*, Cheshire, Melbourne, 1970.

125 Geoffrey Bolton, "Two Pauline Versions," in Prasser et al, *The Menzies Era*, p. 42.

126 Dr Herbert Coombs, quoted in "The Menzies I knew," *The Age*, 20 December 1974.

127 Despite Labor's extravagant promises "Menzies refused to answer Evatt or to outbid him" – Robert Manne, "History repeats Evatt's bid," *The Australian*, 24 February 1996.

128 Ergas and Pincus, "The Wealth of the Nation," p 147.

129 Will Sanders, "Aboriginal Policy," in Prasser et al, *The Menzies Era*, p 264

130 *Report of the Joint Committee on Constitutional Review*, Commonwealth Government Printer, Canberra, 1959,

131 Section 127: In reckoning the numbers of the people of the Commonwealth, or a State or other part of the Commonwealth, aboriginal natives shall not be counted.

132 Sanders, "Aboriginal Policy," p. 271.

133 See Menzies' addresses in Starr, *The Liberal Party of Australia*, p. 82, 104

134 Menzies' addresses in Starr, *The Liberal Party of Australia*, p. 82, 104.

135 Margaret Fitzherbert, "Courting the women's vote is nothing new – Menzies started it," *The Age*, 16 November 2007; Margaret Fitzherbert, *Liberal Women: Federation to 1949,* Federation Press, Sydney, 2004.

136 Maximillian Walsh, "Menzies was right, after all," *Sydney Morning Herald*, 21 December 1995.

137 Menzies, *The Forgotten People*, p.3.

138 Robert Menzies, *Election Policy Speech*, 1963.

139 Strangio et al, *The Pivot of Power*, p, 18.

140 John Murphy, "Social Policy and the Family," in Prasser et al, *The Menzies Era*, p. 223.

141 John Dedman MP, *Commonwealth Parliamentary Debates*, House of

Representatives, "Commonwealth and State Housing Agreement Bill 1945," 2 October 1945 p. 6265.

142 Alistair Greig, *The Stuff Dreams are Made Of: Housing Provision in Australia 1945-1960*, Melbourne University Press, Melbourne, 1995, p. 98.

143 See Robin Boyd, *The Australian Ugliness*, Cheshire, Melbourne, 1960 and for a critique see Hugh Stretton, *Ideas for Australian Cities*, Griffin Press, Adelaide, 1970, pp. 7-23.

144 Murphy, "Social Policy and the Family," p. 235.

145 Ibid., p. 237.

146 Ibid.

147 Leslie Crisp, *Australian National Government*, Longman, Melbourne, 1973, p. 187; This section paraphrases Crisp's comments as in Greig, *The Stuff Dreams are Made Of*, pp. 98-99.

148 Nethercote, "A man to reassure Australia," 1994.

149 This section acknowledges: Graeme Starr, "On the Political Side," in Nethercote, *Menzies*, pp. 57-76.

150 Department of Prime Minister and Cabinet, *PM Transcripts, Press, Radio and Television Conference given by Sir Robert Menzies*, Parliament House Canberra, 20 January 1966

151 Menzies, "Schools and War," *Forgotten People*, p. 157.

152 Ian Wilkinson et al, *A History of State Aid*, p 21.

153 Menzies MP, *CPD*, HR, 26 July 1945, pp. 4612-4621.

154 Ibid., p. 4618.

155 Ibid., p. 4619.

156 Susan Davies, *The Martin Committee and the Binary Policy of Higher Education in Australia*, Ashwood House, Melbourne, 1989.

157 Martin, *Robert Menzies Volume 2*, pp. 398-399.

158 Gough Whitlam, Address to Harvard Club, 1973, reported in Tim Dodd, "Christopher Pyne plays education reformer," *Australian Financial Review*, 12 November 2012.

159 Scullin, Curtin, Chifley and Calwell were Catholics, while Bert Evatt and Whitlam weren't.

160 Mark Lyons, "Sectarianism," in Galligan and Roberts, *The Oxford Companion to Australian Politics*, pp. 535-537.

161 Menzies, *The Measure of the Years*, pp. 92-3.

162 Menzies, *Liberal-Country Party Election Speech*, 12 November 1963.

163 See Ian Hancock, *John Gorton: He did it his way*, Hodder Headline, Sydney, 2002, p. 103.

164 Ibid., p. 104.

165 Ibid., p. 97.

166 Taylor, *Class Wars*, pp. 33-34.

167 Bill Hayden, *Bill Hayden: An Autobiography*, Harper Collins, Melbourne, 1996, p. 135.

168 Part of this section is drawn from Scott Prasser and John Warhurst, "Uncertainty masked prosperity," in *The Week-End Australian*, 8-9 October 1994.

169 Henry Kissinger, *Diplomacy*, Simon & Schuster, New York, 1994, p. 137.

170 Department of Prime Minister and Cabinet, *PM Transcripts, Press, Radio and Television Conference given by Sir Robert Menzies*, 20 January 1966.

171 Douglas, "Rethinking History," 2014.

172 Alex Josey, *Lee Kuan Yew: The Critical Years 1971-78*, Vol 2, Marshall Cavendish International, 1980 – republished in 2013, p. 532.

173 Robert Murray, "Altered Statesman," *The Australian*, 7 January 1993.

174 Prasser and Warhurst, "Uncertainty masked by prosperity," 1994.

175 Jack Richardson, *Patterns of Australian Federalism*, Research Monograph No 1, Centre for Research on Federal Financial Relations, ANU, Canberra, 1973, pp. 114-122.

176 Parts of this section is based on Elaine Thompson's "Menzies and the Public Service," paper presented to, *Menzies Era Conference*, ANU and USQ, ANU, Canberra, 10-11 November 1994 – quoted with permission. Also, used was Beverley Castleman, "Contrasting Styles: 1939-41 and 1949-66," paper presented to, *Menzies Era Conference*, 10-11 November 1994.

177 Thompson, "Menzies and the Public Service," 1994.

178 Gerald Caiden, *The Commonwealth Bureaucracy*, Melbourne University Press, Melbourne, 1967, p. 64.

179 See Scott Prasser, *Royal Commissions and Public Inquiries in Australia*, LexisNexis Butterworths, Sydney, 2006, pp. 154-155.

180 Menzies quoted in Thompson, "Menzies and the Public Service," 1994.

181 Prasser, *Royal Commissions*, pp. 46-54.

182 Elaine Thompson, "The Boyer Committee on Public Service Recruit-

ment in Retrospect," *Australian Journal of Public Administration*, Vol 48 No 2, September 1989, pp. 145-154.

183 See Patrick Mullins, *Tiberius with a Telephone: The Life and Stories of William McMahon*, Scribe, Melbourne, 2019, pp. 138-139.

184 Les Bury, Minister for Air was sacked in July 1962 for contradicting the Government's (and in particular McEwen's) views on the impact of Britain joining the European Economic Community. A year later he was reappointed to the housing portfolio.

185 Wallace Brown, *Ten Prime Minsters: Life Among the Politicians*, Longueville Books, Double Bay, 2002, p. 29.

186 Ibid.

187 Brian Costar, "The Politics of Coalition," in Prasser et al, *The Menzies Era*, p. 108.

188 John Nethercote, "Menzies and the Institutions of Government and Parliament," in Nethercote, *Menzies*, p. 335.

189 Brown, *Ten Prime Ministers*, pp. 28-9.

190 Kenneth Davidson, "A lesson for Keating in the Menzies years," *The Age*, 29 October 1994.

191 Prasser and Warhurst, "Uncertainty masked by prosperity," 1994.

192 Gough Whitlam, "Australia's Prime Minister," *The Australian*, 20 December 1974.

193 Colin Hughes, "Menzies II," in *Australian Prime Ministers: 1901-1972*, Oxford University Press, Melbourne, p. 160.

194 Quoted in Kevin Perkins, *Menzies*, p. 240.

195 John Howard, *The Menzies Era: The Years that Shaped Modern Australia*, HarperCollins, Sydney, 2014.

196 Clive James, "Review of J.W. Howard's The Menzies Era," *Times Literary Supplement*, 15 April 2015.

197 Ibid.

198 Robert Menzies, For Press: "Resignation of Prime Minster – Statement by Sir Robert Menzies," PM No 11/1966, 20 January 1966.

www.ingramcontent.com/pod-product-compliance
Lightning Source LLC
Chambersburg PA
CBHW060554100426
42742CB00013B/2550